Stop Pushing String:
Getting Decisions Made with the Five Languages of Business

Norsemen Books

In memory of Mariann Stuart

Contents

Foreword

A long time ago, someone told me that getting a decision made can be as frustrating as pushing string. Think about it – if something is connected to you by a string, you can move it toward you by pulling on it. However, you cannot move the object by pushing on the string...it goes nowhere.

In the case of decision making, unless your communication pulls the decision maker in, anything you say will be like pushing string. Let me explain: decision communication is about truly connecting with the recipient (an internal or external client), understanding the way they think, and delivering information in a way that makes decisions as easy as possible for them.

My experiences from both inside and outside companies have boiled down to a few simple ideas about getting decisions made, and the relationships that develop from the way decisions are communicated:

- One of the best ways to become a "decision whisperer" is to deliver information supporting a decision in a way that is clear to the recipient.
- In order to deliver information in a way that is clear, the communicator that understands their

client's culture of decision making and the language that goes with it has a distinct advantage. Those who do not make the effort to think and communicate in the same way as their clients spend a lot of time pushing string.

- Many believe that providing more data makes it easier for decisions to be made. This is simply not true.

The concept of the Five Languages of Business came to me through situations in my own career life. I spent a lot of time getting people to make the decision to spend a lot of money, make a significant change or do something they weren't quite prepared to do.

When decisions were needed I communicated data for the decision in a way that made total sense to me. I often spoke in construction or real estate language to someone who might think in a finance way. That caused a lot of re-work, re-communication, and took a lot of time. While it taught me a lot, it probably frustrated my internal clients to no end. I am glad they were patient with me!

In the career following all that decision making, I observed consultants struggling to communicate in a language that helped their clients make a decision to buy their services or to spend money. I actually had the same issue in my consulting work. Consultants, including me, usually made one of two mistakes: communicating data instead of information to their client, or putting that information in terms of what was important to the consultant rather than the client. Or both.

For definition's sake in this book, "data" is the statistics, figures, or other raw facts underlying information. "Information" is defined as the focused and summarized data specific to the decision to be made.

A real life story about information vs. data: in my life as a client I once had a consultant give me a giant stack of research data as a method to influence me to make the decision of going with a certain material. I couldn't make heads or tails of it, forcing a lot of back and forth until the information relevant to the decision finally surfaced.

Data rather than information forces recipients to sift through the mountains of details to determine what is important for the decision they are being asked to make. When information isn't focused nor in a language that has meaning for the client, they then struggle to figure out the important parts of the information and how it relates to the decision at hand. This struggle is what frustrated my clients – and I am sure it frustrates others.

This book is a compilation of what I have learned and continue to learn (as both an internal employee and external consultant) about the advantages of knowing the Five Languages of Business, and how they support great decision conversations. Additionally, the practice of learning your client's language opens the opportunity to learn the client and deepen the relationship with them.

The concepts here are delivered with a project as their backbone to serve as an example of all the places the Five Languages of Business can be learned and used. The Five Languages are not limited to project management as they can be used in a myriad of situations. The key is that they can lead you to better understanding of how the person across from you thinks.

All of the scenarios and activities are designed for use whether you are an internal or external resource and can be used in their entirety or piece-by-piece. Chances are you might be in the middle of a project and can't start from the beginning. Don't worry! Just pick a spot in the book similar to where you are and go from there.

Introduction

The Five Languages of Business give you the opportunity to speak and think in a way that communicates what is important to decision makers in the way they hear it best. If you can speak the Five Languages of Business, you are thinking like your client.

Everyone speaks a business language, and they hear decision points and requirements best in whatever their language is. Beware! No one person in a company speaks just their language, so gauging their primary language and understanding what else is needed is critical.

The Five Languages of Business are **Vision, Finance, Execution, Change**, and **Strategy**. Note: the examples of the types of information to include in the conversation are partial. What you offer will be further nuanced by what is important to the specific decision maker. This will vary from person to person and company to company.

Vision

This is the language the Chief Executive officer (CEO) speaks. A CEO sees any decision or need for how it contributes to, or impacts, forming or fulfilling the company's vision, the demands of evangelizing the business, as well as the risks of addressing or ignoring a problem or opportunity.

Addressing risk, financial implications, and how the solution supports the strategic vision is the best way to get your point across to the CEO. They may also rely on the advice of their Chief Operating Officer (COO or President) and Chief Financial Officer (CFO) regarding actual resolution. So, articulating elements that a CEO cares about is a strategic benefit, enabling them to keep the decision in terms of what is important to them.

Finance

This is the primary language for the Chief Financial Officer (CFO) and a secondary language for the CEO. When you think in financial terms and are fluent in this language, you are able to reach someone with a keen mind for numbers and the relative application to the bottom line.

They want to know the financial impact to the big picture and will need information to weigh the risk of things. Communicating with the CFO needs to encompass current and future spend as well as savings. Connecting spend to revenue (as appropriate) is desirable, as is putting actions and results in financial terms.

Execution

The language of **Execution** is anchored in how to get things done in the most effective way possible. The Chief Operating Officer (COO) needs to keep the day-to-day business running smoothly. So, speaking to results and how they will make the business run better is a great way to get their attention.

The COO translates **Strategy** to **Execution** – if you can connect the plan with the way to get it done you will keep them happy. Many COOs are versed in Six Sigma and messages delivered in terms of improvement (either continuous or one-time) will help them make decisions. Answering the question, "How?" is a great way to engage the COO.

Change

This language addresses shifts and engagement needed at all levels to make changes successfully. The decision maker is most likely the Chief Information Officer (CIO) as change management often resides in Information Technology. If your organization has a Change or Program Management Office (CMO/PMO) the decision maker could also be there.

Additionally, Human Resources (HR) often has responsibility for change management. The change executive, no matter where they sit, is interested in the plan and information for any of the groups affected or involved with changes created by the decisions or work.

Of particular interest will be how to create the desire for change and reinforcing it once the change has been made. They want to see a sense of urgency and continued momentum as well as understanding what communications and collaboration are needed. A great way to engage them is to answer the questions, "Why?" and, "What's in it for the employee?"

Strategy

This language is about planning and approach. It permeates all business conversations. All decision makers will speak this language in some form. When you speak and think strategically, you pose ideas and solutions in terms of "Why?", "Who?" and "When?"

Although these sound like execution questions, they are actually planning questions. To best communicate on a strategic level, any level of decision maker will want to know the answers to these questions, along with how those answers fit with the strategic vision of the company.

Visually, you might see the languages fitting together like this:

Remember, no one person speaks just one language – they may have a primary they default to, and everyone speaks in multiple languages throughout their career. One way to tease out how the decision maker thinks and what language they speak is by putting things in terms of options and consequences (as mentioned above in the CFO persona).

A former manager of mine taught me this: options are all about what can be done, including the bad ones (they are still options - don't ever forget that). Then look at the options and describe the consequences in the particular language of the person you have to deliver the choices to. For example, putting options in project management language then translating them to a vision, financial, execution, change, or strategic language helps hone your ability to translate for the receiver.

Learning these languages takes time, practice, patience, and no small bit of desire. The great part of understanding them is that once known, they can become a regular part of how you operate. Application of the languages is purely situational as well.

Maybe you have a great relationship with the decision maker you are working with and communication seems relatively easy. That's great – you have learned their language during the development of your working relationship! But what if they leave or you are assigned to a different decision maker? Do you know how to work with *them*? Will they operate the same way? If you know the Five Languages you can confidently approach any decision making situation.

Chapter 1 – Project Management and the Five Languages

A great place to learn and practice the Five Languages is in managing projects. Project managers (PMs) not only have to watch all the elements and activities of a project, they need to form the relationships that ensure promises made are promises kept.

The average person might say that project management is getting tasks done on a schedule and making sure everyone is doing what they are supposed to. Looking a little deeper, project management is actually a relationship-based discipline focused on making sure critical promises are made – and kept – during a project. This in turn requires knowing how to drive for promises and support the decisions that keep them.

When preparing to start a project I often coach people to ask the following questions. You will see these and the answers to them in the following chapters:

1. What needs to be done (in the way of activities) moving forward?
2. What has already been done (where are they in the process) so far?

3. What decisions need to be made or what decisions have already been made and who made them?
4. What difficulties might occur in getting decisions made or was experienced in getting previous decisions made?
5. What languages does your decision maker/client speak?

Communication is the key to managing the decisions and promises a project requires. This is where the Five Languages come in – useful tools for getting projects done and promises kept with the most support and understanding possible. I used to believe project managers were born, not made; I've been proven wrong over time. Project management skills can absolutely be learned. They who master the art of managing promises and relationships, along with the communication that supports them, are the ones who shine.

Lack of project success is typically a combination of incomplete communication (leading to promises not being kept), and process issues (resulting in activities not being completed). Project management as a process is relatively simple to execute. The communication needed to keep the process moving is much more subtle and complicated.

Perhaps there is a business problem needing some attention. You might use the Five Languages to approach the questions like this:

- **What has already been done?** Perhaps the problem has been ongoing and previous attempts to solve it have been unsuccessful. The language of **Finance** can outline the problem in terms of the impact to the financial health of the organization, for any previous attempts to solve the problem in other ways, or the cost to the bottom line to ignore the problem further. This discussion could result in the promise of funding for a project to solve the problem.
- **What needs to be done?** In terms of project activities and promises, the language of **Vision** allows decision makers/stakeholders to understand how a problem impacts the ability to realize the company's strategic direction or vision. This might lead to a promise of resources for a project to solve the problem.
- **What decisions have been made?** In taking a look at how previous decisions influence those in the future, the language of **Strategy** can speak to the plan for getting the business problem solved and how that fits with the overall strategic vision of the company. A conversation in this language can result in the promise of stakeholder commitment and engagement.

- **What decisions will be needed?** There will be a myriad of decisions to be identified, including resources needed to execute the project. The language of **Execution** centers discussions on the "how" and "who" of the resources needed and if the project will lead to an increase in effectiveness or productivity.
- **What challenges to decision making might arise or have already been experienced**? Looking back at challenges to decision making can help you identify where they may need to use a different language or hone their skills in the language they did use. Using the Five Languages isn't the only solution to decision-making challenges. However, it is a big tool in reducing those challenges.
- **Which languages are needed?** Identifying challenges to decision making is one of the best ways to figure out which of the Five Languages might prevail. Depending on who you are working with and for on the project, you may need to speak one (or all) of the Five Languages. Is the problem that needs attention one of financial risk? Is the project to solve it going to increase effectiveness or create the need for organization-wide change? You get the picture.

Bad communication creates a loss of engagement at all levels. Loss of engagement results in not achieving the desired results of the project, which could mean a lot of money and a lot of effort spent getting nothing done. There is also the people piece – loss of employee engagement is costly in terms of productivity and turnover.

There are many, many examples of project managers who damaged their team because of lack of communication to drive decisions. Nobody wants to work with them again because of the experience, so these PMs become ineffective and less valuable to the company.

In my experience, about 90% of the project managers I've come in contact with need help understanding who they are talking to and how they are talking to them. In contrast, 10% of project managers I've met have a great balance of the tactical strength of managing promises with knowing what to say, as well as when and how to say it.

Project managers with this balance are highly valuable and are in high demand. A reputation built on getting things done in full collaboration with everyone, where everyone succeeds and can celebrate that success, is huge.

Communication is the focus of this book and you will find this repeated throughout as you read. How can the Five Languages help? The Five

Languages give a foundation to clear communication and are so critical to ensuring promises are kept.

Individuals using the Five Languages to understand information and translate it drive the decisions that enable promises to be kept. They have a high potential to engender a lot of trust from their decision makers. With an understanding of the Five Languages, those decision makers don't have to worry about translating what is said into a language they understand best. When you can rely on someone to think and talk in the Five Languages to guide the promises critical to success, it's as if a heavenly choir sings.

Chapter 2 – The Five Languages and Identifying Business Problems

Project Questions

What has already been done?
What needs to be done?
What decisions have been made?
What decisions will be needed?
Challenges to decision making?
Languages needed?

I mentioned in Chapter 1 that a great place to learn and practice the Five Languages is in managing projects. Projects have their origins in business problems. These projects might also be referred to as strategic initiatives. The challenge of having the right project – where the right decisions and promises are made – comes in making sure of: 1) what and where the problem is, 2) who is affected by it, 3) if the problem should be solved, and 4) what solution to communicate.

Going back to the basic questions asked in Chapter 1, there is a small set of more strategic activities that answer the questions "what needs to be done?" and "what decisions are needed?"

What needs to be done? Before everyone goes running off to create a project to solve a problem or complete a strategic initiative, there are another three questions that will begin to clarify the problem and a proposed project. Invest the time to ask and determine the answers to the following (hopefully these questions are being asked at the strategic planning level as well!):

1. What is the problem?
2. Why is it a problem?
3. What happens if we do nothing?

The first question is the most critical for a couple of reasons. First, it exposes you to the thinking and language decision-makers use (a great way to start determining the way they think). Assuming the problem owner is a decision-maker in this case, the nature of the question supports the use of one or more of the Five Languages to explain the situation. The question "What is the problem?" drives the problem owner to describe the problem in detail: in a visionary, strategic, financial, execution or change related way.

Coming to an understanding that the problem is really a problem will also give keys to the culture of decision making and who has the authority to say something is a problem in the first place. If there is agreement that the problem is really a problem, the second question has the decision maker digging deeper to explain the *present* effect of the problem on one or all of the following:

- Realizing the company's vision (**Vision**)
- Financial health of the organization (**Finance**)
- Effective operations now and in the future (**Execution**)
- Change needed in the organization to fix the problem (**Change**)
- Strategic plans in place (**Strategy**)

What decisions are needed? The third question leads the decision maker to talk about the *future* effect of not solving the problem in terms of the Five Languages. If discussions have led to the determination that the problem really is a problem and why, then looking at what happens if nothing is done will lead to the decisions needed to solve the problem.

Conversely, perhaps an issue has a short-term effect; if it is looked at through a future lens there is little or no impact to the business. The handy bit about these questions is they can help clarify an issue that looks like a problem and isn't, preventing the costs of a large project to solve something everyone might agree is better left alone. Not every problem needs a solution!

Armed with the above information, let's take a look at the example business issue: a sales cycle problem. For the remainder of the book, we will be working on a problem in the sales department at a fictitious company called Desk. They deal in office furniture and they sell their product globally.

The problem is that the sales cycle at Desk is very long. Sales reps manage both the sales conversations and the contracting process. The concern is that it is taking longer and longer to get contracts in place so Desk can ship their product and recognize the revenue associated with it. Customers are starting to complain that it takes forever to get the product, an indication that Desk might lose the customer and therefore, their market share will shrink.

Sales reps are struggling because their commission structure is based on contract completion, not the close of the sale before the start of the contract process. The sales manager (also a decision maker) has been talking about the issue for quite a while and the need to solve it. There are some in the company that don't see the sales cycle as a problem – after all, the contracts get signed, don't they? Products get shipped and revenue comes in, right?

What is the Problem?

In order to get alignment that the problem is a problem to solve, the sales manager can use one or more of the Five Languages to explain what the problem is:

1. In the language of **Vision**, a long sales cycle delays revenue realization which, perhaps, is required to fulfill the CEO's vision of growth into another market.
2. In the language of **Finance**, revenue delays cause cash flow issues, profit delays and other bottom line problems.
3. In the language of **Execution**, delays in revenue can equate to delays in resourcing other initiatives, which then affects bringing on the right resources at the right time, making for an inefficient operation.
4. In the language of **Change**, if the sales cycle problem is to be solved, there may be change needed. What would be in it for the sales reps?
5. In the language of **Strategy**, if Desk wants to keep their customers, which in turn keeps revenue robust, the time to finish contracts needs to shorten.

How does any of this give insight to the decision-making culture? Let's say the sales manager is relatively new to the company. Conversations in any of the languages will give insight on what things are most heavily considered when deciding something is a problem.

The sales manager will also start to understand who has the most influence in decision making and what language they primarily speak (this will shift at any given time – the benefit to knowing the Five Languages is that they are a great starting place to figure out where deciders/influencers are no matter what changes).

Why Is It a Problem?

Recall that this question is about the present impact of the problem. From the conversations around the first question, the sales manager has gotten a sense of how decisions are made at Desk. It turns out that the CEO is very set on growing into other markets (his Vision) and is frustrated by how slowly this is happening.

The COO has seen the growing inefficiencies around resourcing and her ability to hire as needed, losing some competitive advantage by not getting the right employees for Desk's future (**Execution**). Underlying all of this are the CFO's concerns around the bottom line health because of delays with revenue. This is the group that will be most involved and influential in the decisions about rectifying the problem. However, assume that there are still some influential parties that aren't quite convinced the problem needs to be solved.

To go a bit deeper into the example, from the first question, the sales manager has gotten agreement that the sales cycle length is too long. Through asking the first two questions and posing the present impacts in terms of the applicable language, Desk's leadership has realized contract negotiations are lengthy because of the contract itself, not because the sales people don't know how to negotiate a contract. The contract hasn't kept up with how Desk sells or delivers its products. Now we're getting to the root cause – a problem with the contract, not sales.

What Happens If We Do Nothing?

Recall that this question is about future impacts. Looking at the answer to this question from an execution point of view, the "people" impact might be huge. In the language of **Execution**, Desk might lose good sales people or they will disengage because of the challenge of getting a contract done. Both of these scenarios lower productivity, which impacts the bottom line, and so on, up the chain.

This leads to an outline of the impacts of doing nothing in financial terms. In the language of **Finance**, the CFO will want to know: Will there be money lost? Will the loss of good sales folks result in an increase in hiring and training costs in the future? What does that do to other planned expenditures – will other departments have to go without something to allow for the increase?

An added benefit to conversation around the last question is it assists in identifying the benefits of fixing the problem. For example, if the problem with the contracts is solved, the sales cycle shortens. If the sales cycle shortens, then revenue is realized faster and company goals can be met earlier. The languages of **Vision** and **Finance** come into play here.

If a project is agreed upon to make changes to the contract, the language of **Change** will be necessary to describe why the change is needed and why now, as well as what the benefits of change are to the employees. A project will also add conversations with the CFO around the cost of the project versus the benefits of having the problem solved (return on investment (ROI)).

In the language of **Execution**, the COO will want to understand how the project will be done, when it will be done, and what resources it will take. Using the language of **Strategy**, how does this problem and its solution affect the plans for realizing Desk's overall vision of growth?

The three problem identification questions above will help you dig to find the real issue when looking at a problem. Sometimes it takes a bit of time – a day, or even a week or two, to answer the three questions. The time invested in this activity will certainly reap benefits in learning how decision makers think and make decisions about pointing resources at the right activities. You will start to identify different people's primary and secondary languages as well. Additionally, you will also be able to identify if the problem really is a problem, why it's a problem and what happens if nothing is done.

Afterthought: Problem Persistence

You might be wondering if there is ever an occasion where there's a problem and by fixing that problem the original problem remains or a larger problem occurs. Think about the example we are working with: the first identification of a problem was a sales cycle that took too long.

It appears there is a problem in sales. The company may have thought that perhaps salespeople weren't good at sales and the solution might be training of some form. Maybe there was a problem with the technical systems that the sales people use. The solution could be identified as a systems upgrade.

Since you already know that the problem was revealed to be with the contract negotiation time, it may be obvious that had sales training been implemented the problem would still exist. The same could be said for the systems upgrade. Both solutions would have had some results, just not the result needed.

Expenditures would have been made and the root problem would still exist. Asking the three problem identification questions helps get to the root cause and confirm you are looking at the right problem to solve.

Chapter 3 – Setting Up a Project

Project Questions

What has already been done?
What needs to be done?
What decisions have been made?
What decisions will be needed?
Challenges to decision making?
Languages needed?

To review, the sales manager at Desk has worked through the three problem identification questions to get agreement that there is a problem. That agreement has been made with the CEO, COO and CFO using the languages of **Vision**, **Execution** and **Finance**. Moving forward, a project to look at the contract issues experienced by Desk's sales reps will be initiated.

In order to get ready for the project, the previous questions will need to be answered. First, since this is the beginning of the project, the answer to "**What has already been done?**" on the project is simple. Nothing, except to decide that there is a problem. No project work has taken place.

The same applies to "**What decisions have been made?**" None, except that there will be a project. The answers to these two questions might be different had a project started and gone off the rails!

However, no matter the state of the project, the languages to guide the answers are still the Five Languages.

When approaching the start of a project, a few things need to be figured out and decided upon. These include what the project will be and entail, who has a stake in the outcome (stakeholders), and what roles are needed. As to the languages needed, that will depend on a few things. Let's look at them.

Options and Consequences

With the problem identified, there will be, hopefully, a myriad of options to solve the problem. Each option comes with at least one consequence, good or bad. You will want to evaluate them all. As mentioned in the introduction, options and consequences is a great method to help get decisions made and a superb place to practice the Five Languages.

The method of options and consequences takes into consideration every option available to solve a problem or make a decision, even the "bad" ones. Bad options can be viewed as doing nothing or doing something unpopular. Every option is an option.

The consequences of the option put in terms of any

of the Five Languages helps the decision maker sift through the alternatives and come to a decision. Working with the decision maker in this way can help surface any worries they have about the decision. These worries translate to consequences and get all the impacts of the options out in the open.

For example, maybe one of the options for solving Desk's problem of contracts causing a long sales cycle is to go to outside legal counsel to rewrite the contract. Since the legal department reports to the COO, the consequences (good and bad) can be posed in the language of **Execution**. It may be that using outside counsel frees up legal to work on other things while managing the changes to the sales contract. In other words, it is an efficient use of resources in a busy world.

Another consequence to using outside counsel might be the cost of using an attorney to make the changes rather than review changes made internally by legal. This might lead to including the language of **Finance** – what is the financial impact of this option? In the language of **Execution**, the option might be stated in terms of resource impacts and availability.

For all options, there are consequences for choosing them or not choosing them. Consequences can be communicated well through use of the Five Languages and will set the answer to "What needs to be done?" In this case, what needs to be done is the project scope.

Identifying Stakeholders

A subset under the category of "What decisions need to be made?" is "Who will make the decisions?" Once agreement has been reached that a problem really exists and should be solved, project decision makers need to be identified.

Decision makers fall into the category of stakeholder although stakeholders are not always decision makers. A stakeholder is typically defined as a person with an interest or concern in the outcome of a project and its impact on the business. In the case of Desk's problem (the long sales cycle and contract problem) some stakeholders will be those who have an interest in shortening the sales cycle.

Think about this: a sales rep could be a stakeholder as they have a distinct interest in getting their commissions faster. However, they will not be the ones *making* the decision although they might advise the decision makers. It is important to not overlook identifying the various stakeholders (decision makers, business owners, etc.) who will participate in solving the problem. The confusing part is that there may be a myriad of people who seem like stakeholders.

Here is a thought on a sales rep being a stakeholder. In addition to their very personal interest in faster commissions, remember that at Desk, they are the ones who actually negotiate contracts with clients. They will want to make sure changes to the contract are understandable and address any issues the clients have with them. In other words, the sales reps will need to ensure the contract supports their ability to speak in the Language the client speaks. All the better for a quick buy decision. And you thought the Five Languages were just for internal use, didn't you?

We know from the stated example there is a problem with the sales cycle resulting from the way contracts are written and must be negotiated. It would be reasonable to believe that the legal and sales departments as well as the CEO, CFO and COO are primary stakeholders in the project. From the discussions involving the three questions, you have most likely had a chance to begin to understand the decision-making culture of the company and get a sense of the Languages of each of these stakeholders.

Taking a look at the primary stakeholders, the CEO speaks the language of **Vision**, the CFO the language of **Finance**, and the COO the language of **Execution**. What languages do legal and sales speak?

Legal will most likely speak some form of the languages of **Finance** and **Vision** involving risk to the financial health or realizing the vision of the company.

Sales may speak the language of **Strategy** – the plan to close more sales once the problem is fixed, for example. Or, what changes to sales strategy will be needed to accommodate the new contracts. Because most likely there will be change as a result of the project to solve the contract problem, the Chief Information Officer (CIO) may need to be involved at some level.

Every one of the stakeholders speaks a different language and you, as the PM, are going to need to know how to communicate with them in their own language.

Since you are at the very beginning of a project at this point, a key approach is to understand not only what language a stakeholder speaks but how the stakeholders and members of any team communicate (what systems, how often, etc.). A great set of simple questions (whose answers will be used later) are:

- How do you like your communications to come to you? (Email, phone, fax, letter, stone tablet, etc.)
- What day of the week is best for project communications?
- What time of day is best for project communications?
- What information do you typically need to make decisions? (this is directed more at the information than the language - for example, financial reports or schedules)

You may ask these out loud or you may carry them in your head and use them as guides to collect information while you are listening to stakeholders. There is an adage: *You have two ears and one mouth, use them in that ratio.*

Communication is so dependent on understanding, and listening is the key to understanding what your stakeholders need in order to keep promises. Additionally, the first question helps overcome the assumption that how you prefer to communicate is how everyone likes to receive communications. Don't assume - you know what that does![1]

---

[1] Assumption has often been noted that it makes an *** of you and me.

Getting to the rest of the stakeholders takes spiraling out from the primary group throughout the company and applying one, or more, of the Five Languages appropriately. This will take **Vision**, **Finance**, **Execution**, **Change** and **Strategy** conversations all around the company.

The level of detail in those conversations will most likely vary, depending who you are talking with. In a company, stakeholders may not always be easy to identify, which is why it helps to find the primary stakeholder and ask them who else has a risk in the problem continuing or a stake in solving the problem.

Once you have identified the different levels of stakeholders involved (and the people or departments that would be affected by solving the sales/contract problem) another question comes into play. How do you consider or determine who is going to play a role in being part of the solution? Following on to that, what role do they play? Are there some people that are just spectators while others are highly involved or affected? How do you decide and what are you thinking when you are determining who should be involved?

Project Roles and the RACI

There is a tool that can help set up the conversations needed to decide project roles: a Responsibility Assignment Matrix (typically referred to as a RACI[2]). The term RACI speaks to the designations of the Responsible, Accountable, Consulted and Informed parties in the matrix). The RACI should be discussed and decided on carefully as there can be conflicts with the definitions of each designation.[3]

A RACI is most useful in clarifying roles and responsibilities in cross-functional or departmental projects and processes[4], which the example project

---

[2]Wikipedia definition:
https://en.wikipedia.org/wiki/Responsibility_assignment_matrix

[3] It is incredibly important the team discusses the definition of Accountable / Responsible and get agreement on what the definition is – whether or not it is a definition of R or A that they agree with. The team has to agree. Traditionally, those responsible to do the work are the Responsible role. This role may delegate work to others to assist in getting the work done. Those accountable ultimately answer for the completion of the task/deliverable and delegates the work to those Responsible. They must sign off on the work and they are typically the final approver. There can be only ONE Accountable. In many cases there can be an argument about the definition of Responsible / Accountable depending on the participant's personal view of Responsible. Many times I've been fooled by someone saying they were responsible for the work and they never did a thing. They were also not good delegators so projects with them had a risk of going badly. See **http://racichart.org/the-raci-model/** for more information on RACI diagrams.

certainly fits. The downside of a RACI is the work to remind project team members of the definitions of the designations so they don't start to move into other roles as part of their natural comfort zone or feeling that their role isn't as influential as they would like. All of the work involved in managing a RACI is supported by knowing the Five Languages.

Because the RACI is a matrix, there can be many, many lines of tasks and responsibilities, and each line may, or will, have the Responsible, Accountable, Consulted, Informed designations on them. There are great examples of RACI diagrams available in Excel or on the Internet. In the standard definitions of a RACI, the criteria are as follows:

Accountable is the person ultimately responsible for the work done or decision being made. Assuming you are the PM for the project to work on the contract that is causing the lengthy sales cycle, you will most likely be the Accountable party for the project. In other words, you are accountable for the project being within budget, finishing on time, and accomplishing the desired end results. Not every item on the RACI will need or require an "A" and not all those designated "As" will be the PM.

Hopefully, the CEO (or a stakeholder with the authority to approve decisions on the project) will delegate some authority to you to make project decisions, within a set of boundaries. As the Accountable party for the project, part of your job is to communicate with either the CEO or CFO for approval decisions outside your level of authority. Those communications will most likely take place in the language of **Finance** and **Execution**.

Communications of this type will cover the cost impacts of the project, return on investment (ROI) of the project or cost of changes to the project. In the language of **Execution**, the COO will want to know about schedule and resource impacts that result from the project – especially if part of your project team works for the COO or there is a need to hire more or different resources as a result of the project.

Typically, those **Responsible** are those that do the work. This is a critical role in a project, and there may be many that help complete the work. This is also a place where many people get in trouble with the RACI. The "R" must be the person who gets the work done. A stretch may be that someone on the team will delegate the work to someone else, however, ultimately, the person with the "R" on the matrix is responsible for the work getting done.

In order to get work done, it takes a plan or strategy. Communicating the subtlety of Responsible involves the language of **Strategy**. In deciding who is responsible and for what, it is reasonable to ask if the "R" is going to delegate work, or what the plan is to make sure the work gets done. Often, the "delegator" will want to be Accountable, not Responsible. At this point, the language of **Strategy** can help the project team decide if more detail around functions, tasks, or deliverables are needed in the RACI.

In determining who might be **Consulted**, you will need to look at who must give input prior to a decision being made or task being completed. The primary language for communicating about this role is also **Strategy**. What is the plan to have Subject Matter Experts (SMEs) contribute, approvers review, or involve other parties during the project? For a project that involves changing a process or procedure, the language of **Change** may also be used – especially if the change is highly dependent on people adopting the change.

In the example project for revising Desk's contract, there was a question raised about whether sales reps should be stakeholders or involved in the team. The RACI development is a place to decide what a sales rep's role could or would be on the team. It may be they are the SME that should be consulted when draft changes to the contract are made. They may not be able to decide on implementing the change, however, the change may highly impact their ability to close a sale or accelerate the process

The **Informed** role is anyone who must be informed when a decision is made or work is completed. This role is typically further removed from the project. Therefore, the information they might need could span all of the Five Languages, depending on who they are. For instance, in our project example, one approach may be to rewrite the sales contract. Legal may be the "R" (it has been decided that legal will make the changes to the contract) yet the CFO might be the "I" for this task. The CFO needs to be informed of the decisions on clause changes so they can make sure insurance coverage is not impacted.

This "inform" action uses the language of **Finance** and the conversation will definitely include discussion of risk as a basis for deciding on the changes. And while the CEO may be the ultimate approver of the contract changes, it may be the language of **Strategy** that informs the entire management team of a specific decision on an approach for clients in the new contract so they can plan for communication to clients. The language of **Change** will certainly come into play in letting clients know about changes to the contract – what's in it for them, why the change, why the change now.

Using an American football analogy for the RACI, the Accountable person for the game is the head coach – final decisions and risk are on them. The Responsible role for getting the ball where it needs to go is the quarterback (QB). Breaking the RACI down to individual tasks of the offensive line, each player is responsible for their job.

In essence, the QB is primarily responsible for executing the plays and the rest of the offensive line helps execute the plan of action the play outlines, line by line, in the RACI. Consulted parties are the assistant coaches – subject matter experts who give input. Informed might be the fans, the media, etc. — those who need to be in the know about the game, but aren't specifically accountable for or consulted about the decisions being made.

This is a lot to take in. The key for a successful project is understanding the problem and making sure it is the right problem to solve. Finding stakeholders, defining their roles, and identifying decision makers is also critical.

Using the Five Languages as a basis to listen for what information the decision-makers need and how best to offer it to them enables you to use the right amount of effort to form the project team and ensure everyone understands their role in it.

Chapter 4 – Resourcing

What has already been done?
What needs to be done?
What decisions have been made?
What decisions will be needed?
Challenges to decision making?
Languages needed?

For a review, let's go back to the project questions. Our fictitious company, Desk, has determined that the sales cycle length is a problem through discussions and decisions using the languages of **Vision**, **Finance** and **Execution**. A decision to initiate a project was made, project stakeholders identified and project roles determined through development of a RACI. What's next, you ask?

Let's look at the next decisions and actions:

- Decide if internal or external resources will do the work of the project
- Decide what the external resource will do (scope) and where to find them
- Agree on what Desk will do vs. what the external resource will do
- Decide what skills are essential for the external resource
- Decide where to find/hire the external resource

- If external resources will be used, decide on the process to hire them
- Start that hiring process and identify what part of the project team will participate in that process (see Chapter 3 on project team roles)
- Challenges to decisions:
  - The perception that internal resources are less costly than external
  - Determining the right hiring process for external resources
  - Identifying the people with the authority to make the above decisions (pretty much a constant everywhere you go)

Desk's management agrees that the problem is with the contract the sales reps must negotiate. What hasn't been decided is who will make the changes to the contract (legal department or an outside counsel). What is yet unknown is what will challenge the decision about using internal or external resources for the work of the project.

Accompanying the decision to alter the contract will be other related activities – changing the contract language may create the need for sales rep training on the new contract, education of clients, and/or changes in contracting processes that administrative functions need to be aware of. As a hint, this may require some additional work later.

Internal or External Resources?

Many times, once the work has been done to confirm a problem is something that needs to be fixed, the first reaction is for the company to execute the project internally. After all, it can appear that using internal resources is the lower-cost approach. This can be a subtle challenge to making the decision – managing the perception that it is more effective or efficient to use internal resources.

Consider this, if a company isn't prepared for or doesn't have project managers specifically for the type of project at hand, the work may fall to someone who simply shows the tendencies of project management ("Hey, we need to solve this problem, and you're an organized go-getter").

Given that project management is the art of making sure promises are kept and using the Five Languages to make decisions, as well as keeping track of project activities and status, this organized go-getter could be set up to fail. I've found that companies will stay in denial for a long time about going elsewhere for project help – especially those for whom project management is a core service!

Going back to the problem project – at Desk, the contract used by sales is causing long, drawn out negotiations and lengthening the sales cycle in an unacceptable way. Legal, sales, the CFO, CEO, COO and CIO are all stakeholders and will be involved in the project in some way. Desk's management has decided to use an internal PM to oversee the project based on discussions between the CEO, CFO and COO.

This group lives and breathes the languages of **Finance** and **Execution**. In their discussions they most likely covered items such as risk to other projects from losing a dedicated resource, if funds are available for an external resource to manage the project, or what the company might have to forgo in order to fund the PM.

There isn't yet a decision on using internal or external resources to complete the project. For discussion sake, imagine the company is leaning towards hiring an outside consultant to help with the solution. The discussion on use of internal or external resources for the project is tailor-made for the Five Languages.

Some examples of conversations follow – since use of the Five Languages is completely situational, they may need to be tailored to your own organization. These examples take both positions (internal or external resource):

Speaking to the CEO in the language of **Vision**, hiring an outside resource to modify the contract keeps everyone else in legal best focused on where the company is going. Managing an internal project can distract people and their managers from initiatives propelling the company forward.

Conversely, using an internal resource or resources familiar with the company vision may ensure the project outcome fits with where the company is going. From the big picture financial view, an internal resource may cost less than external and could be less of an impact on realizing the future vision.

In the language of **Finance**, the CFO will be interested in the cost of the external resource vs. the internal resource and return on investment (ROI) of that cost. The ROI discussion will be based both in the savings of time (creating faster revenue recognition and increased sales) as well as the possible efficiencies in using a resource that is focused solely on completing the project. Following the logic from the conversation with the CEO, it may be that an internal resource is actually less costly than an external one. This will figure into the cost comparison.

For the COO, in the language of **Execution**, they will want to know if the skills are available internally, and if not, what barriers exist to getting those skills. Or, say the choice is to dedicate an internal resource to the project. There could be a risk to this, the consequences of which are someone trying to do two jobs at once and not doing either of them well. If they are a critical player in keeping the company running, using an internal person thins out available resources, which could strain operations.

Additionally, if the company lacks PM skills within, an external resource can eliminate the need to hire additional resources for just one project. The opposite argument may be that it is an advantage for an internal resource to execute the project and retain the learning as part of the COO's strategy around skills, growth, or expansion of services.

In terms of **Strategy**, bringing in an outside resource provides an objective 3rd party that has no preconceived notion of challenges within the company, nor any negative reputation that could cause friction during the project. This can help realize the project faster and keep the company concentrating on fulfilling the vision. On the other hand, an internal resource may have the relationships and reputation to overcome any challenges to the project.

Again, the arguments for or against an external resource will be based in the company's available skill sets, nature of the project, timeline, and funds available, to name a few. Other thoughts on external resources which you can use to practice translating among the Five Languages:

- There are no preconceived notions about the politics of the company. There is no promotion at stake, no performance review nor coworkers who may or may not like what the internal PM is doing. (**Strategy**)
- There is a risk that the available internal PM has an existing reputation causing them to be ineffective with decision makers. This can jeopardize the project in many ways, some of which are delayed project approvals or decision makers start to manage the project themselves. The results of a reputation issue can wreak havoc with managing a project. (**Execution**)
- An external resource has to be politically savvy (you don't want a bull in china shop). In most cases they are able to do things differently than internal politics might allow with an internal resource. External resources are often regarded as "the experts from out of town" and companies may tend to listen to them more seriously than an internal resource. (**Execution, Strategy**)
- External resources can also take a little bit more leeway because they have no vested interest other than the successful outcome for the client. There is no attachment to any one particular

person or idea, so they are not politicking inter-nally. (**Execution, Strategy, Change, Vision**)

Finally, be aware that an external consultant/resource can be seen as a subtle (or not so subtle) message that someone's ability has come into question. In that case, the message is about supporting everyone's success from any of the Five Language points of view.

It can be positioned that the external resource is a toolbox that supplements the skills of the internal resource and gives them one more pair of hands to get things done, while supporting the company's vision and financial goals. Using the languages of **Vision, Finance** and **Execution** helps address these concerns.

Hiring External Resources

The use of the question lists and the Five Languages has gotten us through determining the root problem, identifying stakeholders, project roles and deciding on an internal or external resource. The decision has been made to use an internal PM (you) and hire an external consultant to do the work based on the availability of skills, time, and an ROI analysis.

Additionally, from the decision conversations, it has been agreed to have a consultant come in and assess the breadth and depth of the contract issues, as well as any other activities resulting from the changes to the contract. They will also be asked to provide a recommended approach to getting all this done and what it would take to have them implement the recommended approach. The next activities address the skills and qualities needed of the external resource (consultant).

Problem Statement and Outline Scope of Work

Defining the skill set and qualities needed of the consultant is best done through developing a problem statement and an outline scope of work. The problem statement is about the problem you want to solve. An outline scope of work is what you want the consultant to do, at a high level.

Recalling Desk's issue, it has been agreed that there is a problem with the sales contract. The problem statement in this case is pretty simple: the current sales contract appears to be outdated and causes a lot of negotiation back and forth between the company and the clients. Extended negotiations result in a long sales cycle, extending the time it takes to collect payment, which is creating unhappy clients, sales reps and CEOs.

As far as scope of the project, big picture, you want the consultant to assess and confirm the contract problem, then define/recommend an approach to solving it. An assessment of the situation/problem may seem redundant – it could be. However, an outside assessment of the problem will confirm you have hired the consultant to address the *correct* problem.

Keeping the scope at as high a level as possible, be as detailed as possible about what you believe is needed or required. Side note, there are times when a consultant will produce a scope of work based on some discovery they do before actually engaging for the work. No matter which way the scope is developed, it is always good to come in with your own outline of that information.

I stress the "what" because many find it hard not to focus on the "how." If the scope of work is too focused on *how* the consultant should accomplish their work, it increases your risk by dictating their approach. Dictating the approach ("how") can limit the consultant on what they accomplish – mostly because you will see the solution one way. The consultants bring an outside view, innovative ideas and informed recommendations based on all they have done and experienced. **Consultants are hired for their expertise, let them outline *how* best to accomplish what is needed.**

This yin and yang between "what" and "how" is a great place to practice the Five Languages. Whether the scope outline is a group or solo effort, defining the scope of work is a challenge to keep to the "what" of the scope. I've found over my career that most people are naturally "how" people – getting them to define "what" is a struggle.

Going back to the Five Languages, outline the scope for the team from a **Vision**, **Strategy** or **Finance** point of view. Include impacts to the business moving forward or to the financial health of the business of the long sales cycle. Talk about what might happen as a result of modifying the contract, as you see it. In the Five Languages, "what" and "why" are best described with the **Strategy**, **Finance** and **Vision** languages. **Execution** and **Change** languages message the "how" and "who."

For example, Desk management has agreed the contract is a problem, and one discussion point is around the company vision for growth. Delayed revenue stunts the ability to grow at the pace the CEO envisions. "What" the consultant needs to do is to figure out if the Desk team's assessment is correct, what the details of the solution are, and what the approach is to remedy the problem. "How" the consultant does that needs to be, mostly, left up to them.

Ultimately, while it is up to the project team to decide the way the scope is described – there is some inherent risk to telling a consultant how to do the work. If you aren't careful, that approach can lead to additional cost and risk to the company. In the case of specific or uncommon regulations or compliance issues, you may want to dictate how the work is done. Otherwise, let the consultant figure that out – you may get a really creative answer!

Once you land on the problem statement and outline scope of work, the consultant's job is to translate what they can do and how they will do it into the languages you speak. An otherwise great consultant can give a great presentation and make huge errors by framing their proposal from their point of view rather than one of the Five Languages.

A good example is from the technology consulting world: I can't tell you how often I've gotten the technical details of how the software will be built rather than how they plan to approach the project and how it will meet my business need. The consultant was completely excited about the technology, but that conversation left me glassy-eyed and unable to make a hiring decision. It was as if I had asked for the time and gotten a report on how to build a watch.

For Desk's consultant hire, let's include the discussions and answers to the problem questions in Chapter 2 in any information incorporated in the procurement process. Including this information is a great way to educate the consultant to the company's decision making culture. The conclusions made from that exercise can prove invaluable in a couple of ways.

First, to you: the already completed work may shorten what they have to do – it could be they verify that the problem you identified is the problem instead of working on a full blown assessment giving the same answer. Second, to the consultant: it will give them a sense of what things are important to Desk when making a decision, especially if you include what was discussed (risk, cost, ROI, resourcing, impact to long range vision).

Essentially, both this information and the problem statement provides them a view to Desk's culture of decision making – which is important when they need to determine an approach and get you to decide how to implement it. In addition, this helps the consultant start to understand how you will make the decision to hire them!

Developing a scope of work isn't exactly easy. What if we miss something? What if we don't explain it the right way? What if we don't use the right language? What if, what if, what if.

Consultants are hired because they are experts and sometimes when you have a problem, the reason you're bringing in a consultant is that they know or can see something you can't. This can make some people nervous because it's not exactly comfortable to admit you may not know the language of the consultant.

Where Do You Find Them?

If you are starting a project for which you have never hired a consultant, there can be a challenge of where to look for them. Some ideas on where to find them:

1. Professional associations
2. The Internet
3. Peers in your company/past projects
4. Word of mouth from your network

Making the decision on where to go to find them may rest with a procurement department. In Desk's case they don't have one (although I have it on good authority the COO is thinking about forming one to support anticipated growth from fulfillment of the CEO's vision and solving the contracting issue).

Going back to the project team, you will likely need to go over the potential sources for consultants and agree on where to focus efforts. In this case, the conversation with the team can be based partly in the language of **Finance**: what is the value of time spent versus the return on that time? Some of the methods of locating possible consultants are more time consuming than others, and have considerably more risk in finding a consultant that is reputable.

Professional Associations

I know in my part of the world there is a list available of all the professional associations in the area. From there you can research the association and see what kinds of professionals participate in that particular association. Then, talk to the professional associations and see if they can point you in the direction of someone with that skill. I would hope that most professional associations are open to that kind of thing, although they may say they don't recommend specific members. If they do give you a list of some members to talk to, perfect.

At this point you have no idea if the consultant firms are qualified, however, consultants are used to people contacting them and asking if they can do the kind of work needed. (Remember the outline scope of work and problem statement you did earlier?) If the consultant can do the type of work, ask them for a referral or two of work they did that is similar, just to make sure. And then check them out!

The Internet

Depending on how good you are at searching the Internet, you can put in what you're looking for and see what pops up. That may not be the best use of time since searches can be frustrating if you don't know the exact keywords to use. If you do get good results, it's hard to tell from a website how qualified or quality the consultant might be. However, you can still elect to contact them and ask for a reference if the conversation goes well.

Company Peers/Past Projects

The project in this case is an assessment of the sales cycle issues, particularly contract negotiation, assessing any issues and recommending an approach.

An alternate scope piece is having the consultant actually implement the approach to solving the problem. The decision was made to use an outside consultant because internal resources were working on other critical initiatives.

Although internal resources are busy, they may have time to help you with information on similar projects they did in the past. Ask around the company and if another peer PM did a similar project, it could be a fairly simple matter to find out who the consultant was, how they did (if the company keeps a scorecard), and how to reach them.

Word of Mouth/Your Network

One of the best places to find a consultant is going to your network for a referral. Here's the thought: when you ask a consultant for a client referral, they're always going to give you clients that are happy with them. They're never going to give you a client that wasn't.

When you go to your business associates, contacts, or network for recommendations, you will most likely get better ideas and honest feedback about performance. This is why the outline scope of work and problem statement are critical - they serve as your conversation guide.

Note that the word of mouth is from colleagues, staff, and other departments. If I have a contact at a competing company, I may even talk to them. The key to finding a great consultant is knowing someone that knows the consultant, especially if that someone you know has the same kind of business approach you do. This can serve as a gauge of how well the consultant might do for you. Additionally,

I might ask consultants that don't do the needed work if they have a recommendation, especially if that consultant has worked for the company before.

All this research should yield a list of consultants who have passed the first test of good reputation and past clientele that resembles you. The sweet spot of potential consultants is between three and five – this might be hard to get if the work is highly specialized.

In the case of the project Desk is initiating, assessing and solving the sales contract issues, three to five is a reasonable number to shoot for. More than five and you will spend a significant amount of time trying to sort through them once you initiate the hiring process. Let's take a look at that progression.

Chapter 5 – Making the Hire: Requests for Proposals

Project Questions

What has already been done?
What needs to be done?
What decisions have been made?
What decisions will be needed?
Challenges to decision making?
Languages needed?

There were a lot of conversations in the last chapter. The decision was made to use an internal PM and hire an external consultant to look at the problem. A problem statement and scope of work were developed. Lacking a procurement department, Desk's project team made decisions on where to look for the appropriate consultant, found that source, and selected three to five to consider.

Now the time has come to decide on hiring the consultant. Along with all the tactical project management decisions needed, some of the other decisions are:

- What process should be used to hire the consultant?
- How long do we want the hiring process to take?

- There is currently no budget for the project, should one be set before the consultant is hired?
- If a formal process is chosen, who will write all the documentation?
- What requirements need to go in an RFP, if we decide on that process?

Decision challenges:
- **The need for speed:** the contract issue is becoming serious and Desk management wants it solved. The desire to make a fast hire might cloud good judgement around price and expertise.
- **Decision by committee:** the hiring process will most certainly involve a group. Committee decisions are not always the easiest to manage.
- **Writing challenges:** someone needs to write the documentation – not everyone likes that sort of thing.

Let's take a look at hiring processes and making the decision.

Ways to Hire

The problem statement as well as the outline scope of work developed through the activities in the last chapter are helpful no matter what route to hiring a consultant is taken. They are both especially helpful if your in-house consultant hiring (procurement) process is fairly informal. That is, it consists of talking to the consultant for a little bit, calling references and making a decision.

The information in these documents helps make sure you don't miss anything when you are talking to the potential consultant. In a more formal process, all that information and any other you want to impart to the consultant will end up in a document for the consultant to respond to.

Desk has no procurement department to speak of, so the decision on how to hire the consultant will rest on discussing some of the challenges to that decision: the need to hire quickly and the size of the committee used to hire the consultant. The languages of **Execution** and **Strategy** will certainly come to bear on these decisions, along with the risk side of the language of **Finance**.

You have identified around five possible firms to consider for the work. Let's assume they are unknown to Desk, so part of the discussion on how to hire the consultant centers around risk. If the process of hiring the consultant is fairly informal, being that Desk is not familiar with the companies, there is a risk that the outline scope isn't enough for either Desk or the consultant to be sure the work can be done in the time or for the cost agreed to.

This creates higher financial risk than a more formal process. In addition, hurrying to hire a consultant may also result in higher cost because of missing or misunderstood scope. Conversely, an informal hiring process may take less time, which might get Desk to the outcome they are looking for sooner. And, faster turnaround means internal resources will be distracted by the project for less time. This risk/benefit will be of interest to the CFO and COO.

The Formal Hiring Process

With specialized work, there may only be one or two consultants with the skills needed; bringing them in for a problem statement and outline scope review may be the best approach. For Desk's contract revision project, the scope is not that specialized and you've found five possible consultants that appear able to do this work.

The most common approach would be a Request for Proposal (RFP) process. RFPs are a fairly universal method of selecting and purchasing services and they can be complicated to write depending on the services you are trying to buy. The goal of an RFP is to set a level field of competition between viable candidates for the work, as well as to confirm any specific requirements are met. These requirements may be company policies, regulatory compliance, or both.

Although many call the entire process an RFP, it actually breaks down into three or so parts. It may start with a Request for Information (RFI), move to a Request for Qualifications (RFQ)[5] and culminate in a Request for Proposal (RFP)[6]. Note, if your company has a procurement group or is affiliated with Local, State or Federal agencies in some way, there may be a very formal process for hiring a consultant. Every company is different, so please check for your company's situation before you issue any form of an RFx[7].

Generally, each document is used to whittle groups of possible consultants down to the final choice as follows:

- An RFI goes to a large group of consultants to ask if the consultant does the kind of work described in the outline scope and is interested in doing the work in the time needed. An RFI may also ask for business particulars such as size, annual revenue, etc. The RFI responses will whittle down the list of consultants for the next step.

---

[5] An RFQ can also be a Request for Quote depending on the requirements of specific procurement departments

[6] See **www.projectmanagementdocs.com** for sample RFP templates

[7] "x" being a placeholder for I, Q or P

- An RFQ then goes to the list of consultants created by the RFI and presents more detail about business requirements (how long in business, how much does your bank like you, annual revenue over the past few years, etc.). It may also require a list of projects that qualify as example work experience based on the outline scope of work, along with clients the consultant has worked for. RFQs may or may not include the contract vehicle for the consultant and may or may not request pricing. Responses to the RFQ further whittle down the list.

- The RFP then goes to the final list of consultants, usually three or four, and may be very specific about the scope of work, schedule of the work (timeline), deliverables, assumptions, and may include a sample scorecard along with the contract vehicle for the consultant, if it wasn't included in the RFQ. The RFP also requests pricing for the work, the staff that will do the work, including their qualifications, project examples, client references, and may include a set of questions for the consultant to answer based on information given in the RFP.

Here is another way to think about the documents: use an RFI when you don't know the consultants or you have a big list, and you want to narrow the list a little. You can also combine the RFI and RFQ to get all the information and narrow the list faster.

Each of these processes takes time, and your process will depend on how much time you have.

It will also affect the internal budget for procurement, as well as the budget for the consultant. The process is pretty flexible; how flexible depends on the specific policies of your company. You can also bypass the first two efforts and go straight to RFP, although this might take an internal conversation or two.

Getting agreement on the process to hire the consultant will likely use all the languages except **Change** and **Vision**. In terms of **Finance** and **Execution**, there will need to be discussion of the available resources to handle the process – remember that Desk has no procurement department currently.

This conversation might include why the RFP (and not the other two processes) is the most cost effective of the approaches: it is one effort, not three. Included are the benefits of using this process versus the risk of simply interviewing a couple consultants and picking one.

In the language of **Strategy**, the plan of an RFP could be presented as the most expedient. The issue of the long sales cycle affects revenue and cash flow, which in turn could be impacting the realization of the company's vision – you want to get rolling on the solution as quickly as possible while keeping the process fairly formal.

Budget, What Budget?

Now is a good time to talk about budget. Because the contract issue had been largely ignored until it interfered with Desk's CEO's vision for the future, there is no budget for this project. A decision will need to be made whether to set a budget first, or to use the hiring (RFP) process to set the budget. Use the budget conversation as a chance to get in the decision makers' heads about the direction to take.

As with most decisions, there are pros and cons to both ways of setting the budget. Since Desk has never done anything like this, the first tendency might be to want to set a budget first. The CFO will certainly be involved in deciding this, as will the COO, as the project will impact the overall budget of the company along with any operations budget the COO manages. They will be thinking about how to weigh the impact of the project cost on money that has already been allocated to other initiatives or capital purchases.

Remember that the COO is thinking of setting up a procurement department. That information might be handy to know right now – the funds set aside for hiring that department may have to be used to solve this problem. Is there a creative way for the COO to get both? Is there a risk to setting the budget first? If so, what might the risk be?

In this case, in the language of **Finance**, you will want to weigh the risk/benefit of setting the budget at a particular time. Setting the budget first may limit what can get done; conversely, some consultants are eager to hear the budget (they will always ask) so they can tailor their services to give you as much (if not all) of what you need to solve the problem. Setting the budget after the RFP may lead to a big surprise and more decision making before hiring the consultant. From the opposite side, setting the budget after the RFP process gives you a chance to make sure you haven't missed anything.

 If the cost is too high, you might be able to work with the consultant to trim the scope of work down to what will fit in the budget. The CFO and COO will want to consider these risks against the company's overall budget – what they finally decide will tell you a lot about how they make decisions. They might come up with a hybrid of budgets: one might be to estimate something to work against and see where the RFP pricing ends up. This can be offered as an alternative to be able to set a number everyone is comfortable with and deal with anything larger if it materializes.

In the language of **Execution**, you may need to weigh the pros and cons of the possible delays with either approach. It could be faster to figure out a budget first, although there is always the chance negotiations occur because the consultant's price is higher. The COO may be less risk averse than the CFO and wants to wait and see, then deal with the consequences at the future point of RFP pricing.

If the budget has been developed, it will be fairly simple to negotiate the contract if pricing is within the range of the budget. If the budget will be done at RFP pricing, then it will be faster to run the RFP process. Or, the delay might happen at contract negotiation.

All of this has to do with how quickly the pricing information will be available and how much it will cost (in internal labor) to run the process to hire the consultant. All these decisions have impact on how quickly the problem can be solved, which then impacts how quickly the company can recover from the lengthy sales cycle issue. Whew, lots of decisions!

In the case of the project that has evolved from the sales cycle problem, remember that it has been agreed to hire a consultant to perform an assessment and develop a solution and implementation approach. The assessment is to confirm that the length of the cycle is actually due to contract negotiations and that contract negotiations are lengthy because of the contract used. The solution addresses the problem and the implementation approach is how to get the problem solved. It also has been agreed that the decision on who implements the solution will be left until after the consultant figures that out.

The tricky part of this RFP is that it may be difficult to include costs and approach for the implementation in a proposal if those costs depend on the results of the assessment work. In this case, you may end up with a two-part RFP. The first part for the assessment costs which would set the budget for that portion of the work. The second part of the RFP would come after the assessment and would establish the remainder of the costs for the consultant to implement their recommended solution.

The second part would certainly offer an opportunity to make another decision about the cost of internal or external resources executing the solution. Let's assume after all is said and done, the CFO and COO have come to an agreement to let the RFP inform the costs of the project and to commit to a two part RFP process. That is, the consultant will confirm the issue through the assessment and then submit another proposal to develop the solution and implementation recommendation.

The key to a good RFP is to be simple, clear, and concise. Given that a problem statement and outline scope of work have already been developed, the hardest part of the RFP is already done. Sometimes hiring a consultant is much less formal. It might be simply bringing the consultant in to talk about the scope of work and schedule, then letting them respond with a proposal (you always want a proposal from a consultant no matter the process used to hire them).

To get ready for the next steps, keep in mind the scope of work is the basis of the entire RFP process. The best way to make a good consultant hire is to stick to *what* you need done. Let the consultant experts figure out *how* they will get the work done. Recall that Chapter 4 has some great tips on finding the right consultant. Use the appropriate Five Languages with the project stakeholders and other departments to get approval of your plan for using an RFP process to hire a consultant. Now, on to it!

Who Writes It?

Ah, yes, the writing of an RFP. Generally, because the rules are so different at each company depending on size, industry, regulations, procurement processes, the scope of work, etc. there is no one party that always writes an RFP. A best practice is that the PM in charge of the project is the lead writer, supported by procurement. And I do mean *supported* by procurement. As you know, Desk does not have a procurement department – that would come in handy right at the moment.

Let's go back to the group that developed the scope of work. The COO, CFO, legal and sales all contributed to the outline scope and the problem statement – the "what's wrong" and the "what we want the consultant to do." Although there is no formal procurement department at Desk, this group represents most of the skills needed in one (with the exception of sales – they are an important player in another way). Add yourself (the PM) in, and an RFP will be relatively simple to put together.

An RFP can be time consuming to write – the key to getting participation by this group will be in the language of **Vision**. Perhaps it is of value to use this RFP effort as a test bed for how the COO envisions a procurement department running in the future. The CFO and legal will be able to see and experience firsthand how it might work and what benefit it would bring to the company in meeting future growth goals.

When they are available, procurement can help you understand the rules of how the company buys services. However, unless you have a procurement person dedicated to your business unit, they may not know your business well and what you're trying to hire for. Because they are the keeper of the rules, they can sometimes make an RFP complicated.

However, they can also keep the PM out of trouble if there is detailed compliance associated with the business the company is in or based on internal policy. While procurement folks understand overarching compliance requirements, they tend to be circumspect with information. This can put them at odds with the ability to be clear and concise in the RFP. A great procurement person will help the PM navigate the policies around RFPs and make it the best it can be.

Using the aforementioned group as your de facto procurement group could pose the same issues. However, with sales in the mix there will be a firsthand view on the business unit. The sales manager will be involved to provide details of how they work. Something to consider: some of the best RFP sections are written by people who aren't experts in what you are hiring for. They may have a different point of view, and they might ask a different set of questions.

Consider having the person who will negotiate the consultant's contract working with you, whether from procurement or not. At a minimum, have them read the RFP to make sure it is clear and simple. Others that are always helpful on the RFP development team are: subject matter experts, people from other departments outside the one that is the focus of the project (if applicable) or another project manager, if they are available.

Desk's contract problem involves sales and possibly legal, it might be interesting to get a marketing or IT person to sit on the RFP team. The key to an outside department member is their ability to be an objective observer/contributor to the RFP.

Developing the RFP

Although the PM is the lead and most likely the point of contact for the RFP, you won't necessarily do all the work. The writing work can be parsed out as appropriate. Nevertheless, the PM should be the one to set questions to be asked of the consultant, and help develop the specific requirements outlined in the next sections. The art of an RFP is having enough scope information to ask the questions well. Good questions lead to good answers; good answers help lead to a good consultant hire.

The Five Languages are used to confirm scope and requirements with the stakeholders in various ways. You already have agreement that the sales cycle is a problem, and you have spoken with the C-Suite about the risk to realizing the company's vision, and the cost impacts of the problem continuing as return on investment for the project.

Legal is on your team as well, so they can bring compliance requirements into the mix. Their largest concern will be about the risk to the company around the contract to be used with the consultant, as well as any changes to the current Desk sales contract. The latter will be addressed in the implementation stage, although there may be questions to include in the RFP that help legal understand the consultant's ability to modify contracts. These conversations will be in the languages of **Execution** and **Finance**.

Some common discussions center on levels of insurance to be required of the consultants. Some companies require certain amounts or types of insurance and there may be an additional cost to those. The language of **Finance** helps make the decision on the insurance requirements and the value of that insurance against any additional cost that might be incurred.

Another component of insurance may be that the insurance required isn't a type the consultant carries. A common example of this is Theft insurance.

In the past I've seen companies require Theft insurance for a consultant that executed their work remotely. There was no chance that any of the consultant's employees would be anywhere near the client's location to steal anything. The requirement for that insurance was waived since the consultant didn't normally carry it and would have had to buy a policy. And that cost would be passed along to the client.

As the test bed for the COO's vision of a procurement department, the languages of **Execution** and **Strategy** might come into play. The COO will want to understand how you might plan to use or work with procurement on this project, as well as what you estimate the effort to be. This would be especially interesting to the COO if the project was unplanned.

Because you are using the RFP project to determine the budget, assume for the sales cycle/contract example project it is unplanned and prepare to have a resourcing and budget conversation with the COO in the languages of **Strategy** and **Execution**.

Once you have determined who is leading the RFP preparation and you have your procurement partner involved, you can begin to develop the document. Information in the aforementioned RFx documents can be linked and built upon. In general, the following is information asked for in any, or all, of them. Not all companies request all of the information, so use the below as a guide and have the decision conversation with the RFP team (COO, CFO, legal and sales):

- Company structure (corporation, LLC, etc.) and age
- Management team
- Lines of service/business
- Financial history and stability as well as annual revenue (over X number of years)
- Ability to meet insurance requirements
- Issues with contract terms (if the contract is included in the RFP)
- Experience with the type of work in the RFP (by number or type of projects, for example)
- Proposed staff, qualifications to do the requested work, and organization chart
- Point of contact for the project and level of authority within the company
- Client list
- Referrals
- Detailed scope of work
- Schedule of work (timeline)

- Pricing for the scope of work and pricing assumptions
- Deliverables (what am I buying?)
- Payment terms desired (unless dictated by your contract)
- Any other company or experience specific questions

The first goal of the RFP is to understand the potential consultant as a business. As a business, the consultant needs to be stable and established so they can complete the work – there is nothing like having a consultant go out of business in middle of a project!

The underlying goal of the RFP is to get a feel for how they think and work, how they will manage the project for you, how they will interact with you, as well as how well they might know the Five Languages.

In asking for company structure, management team, and point of contact, you are trying to find out ownership shares and get a sense of the decision-making culture of the consultant. For example, if you ask the point of contact about changing something in the project, the goal is to see if you are going to encounter a long process to get the consultant to agree to the change.

You need someone that has the authority to make decisions for the consultants in a timely manner. In terms of the Five Languages, you might ask them to outline how they communicate contract changes. This will give you a sense if they have a grasp on the **Finance** or **Execution** languages.

The financial stability and revenue questions are posed to help get a read on where your project fits in their financial world and if there is any financial risk to you (essential for talking the language of **Finance** with your CFO when getting approval for the project budget). It could be the project you are hiring them for is a very large part of their annual revenue, or they are doing a lot of work for you already.

Many larger companies do not want to hire a consultant where their work for the company is more than 15% of their total annual revenue. This signals that the consultant may be relying on that particular company for a very large portion of their survival.

Think about it this way – if any one company is 15% or more of a consultant's revenue the consultant is vulnerable to failure should any one of their clients stop working with them. This situation can put your company at risk of having the consultant go out of business in the middle of your project.

Schedule, Assumptions, Deliverables

There are a few other things to decide on including in an RFP: schedules, assumptions, or deliverables. Side note: if you are not going to go through the formal RFP process, it is particularly important to get a schedule, pricing assumptions, and deliverables from the chosen consultant. This information helps keep everyone on the same page.

Schedule or Timeline

Schedule will be one of the places that challenges the decisions needed to run the RFP process. Desk management is already feeling pressed by the need to resolve the problem on the sales contract. Although they already agreed to the RFP process, they may want to shorten both the RFP process schedule and the end date of the consultant's work!

Keep in mind, there are two schedules (or timelines) for an RFP. First, the schedule of the RFP process itself. This timeline outlines how long the process will run and when certain deliverables in the process are due (questions from the consultant or actual proposal).

The timeline keeps the process clear for both the consultants and Desk RFP team, as there are activities both will need to engage in. These include asking/answering questions, proposal/response reviews, decision making on the short list, interviews, final decision making, and contracting.

The RFP process timeline plays an important part in the **Strategy** and **Execution** communications with your internal project team about when they will need to be ready to participate and what they will be doing at that time. Recall that the project team's role and responsibilities are included in the RACI matrix discussed in Chapter 3.

The second timeline is that of the actual project work and will be a required deliverable in the consultant's proposal. This is a conversation with the Desk RFP team in the languages of **Strategy** and **Execution**. That is, if they want to shorten the project work timeline, what is the potential impact or risk to the quality of the outcome?

Addressing that urgency between **Execution** and **Strategy** will lead to conversations with the COO about what internal resources are needed, their roles and responsibilities, and confirming that the appropriate resources can be made available. Also, there may be a component of the risk of not having internal resources available. This will drive some decisions on mitigating that risk.

One last thought on setting timelines. If there are any dates the consultant needs to know about where company resources are not available, it is smart to note that in the RFP. For instance, perhaps your company shuts down for the last two weeks of the year. If the project delivery relies on having people available during that week, the consultant would be hard pressed to make it happen with no one in the office.

Having these dates up front sets the project team up for success by allowing them to plan for participants being unavailable. The schedule, combined with the consultant's assumptions, are a great way to understand how the consultant thinks and what they are thinking about.

Assumptions

Because Desk's project team has done a great job of outlining what is needed, the consultants have only to figure out how they are going to get the scope of work done. In doing this, they will make a set of assumptions: how long it takes, who they need to talk to, what it will cost, who on their team they might use.

All of the assumptions they develop will most likely be developed by them in the language of **Strategy** – that is, what is their plan to get this work done? Then, in the language of **Execution**, they will describe *how* they will get the work done. **I believe the assumptions are the most critical part of any consultant's proposal – if you don't get any in the proposal, beware!**

The consultant's list of assumptions helps you understand the thinking of how they got to their approach, their pricing, their staffing model, and their schedule. They are a set of boundaries around their response. Considering the project you want the consultant to undertake, they may assume you are going to want them on-site and therefore will provide a place for them to sit. This is a cost for you to consider.

Additionally, suppose they assume they will have access to your systems for ease of communicating with the internal project team. All of their assumptions help you understand how they think about the scope of work.

One of the most common misaligned assumptions I've seen has been around pricing. Let's say the consultant based pricing on a schedule of twelve weeks. Due to project circumstances the schedule ends up being thirteen weeks instead. A conversation in the language of **Strategy** then takes place about the decision to take an additional week to do the work.

If there were no assumptions about the length of the project then there is no good place to start the conversation and come to an agreement. With assumptions, at least you have a place to start the conversation.

The best consultants walk you through all the assumptions when they submit a proposal. The review includes all the assumptions they made for their pricing, project approach or staffing, so everyone is clear.

Smart consultants never give a proposal without walking their client through it. I would go as far as making it a practice for your projects, as an internal PM, to make sure all consultants walk you through their proposal. If they don't immediately do that, ask for it. If they cannot state their assumptions, walk away, it will be more of a headache than you want.

Assumptions help lay out the basis of thinking behind the scope, timeline and cost – if these things happen, then the project has the best chance of going as outlined. If something varies from the assumptions, then you have the basis of the decision to work from.

Deliverables

End of project deliverables are project knowledge transfer from consultant to the client. Deliverables from the project can be asked for in the RFP – the consultant may offer others or suggest additional. There may not always be deliverables – for Desk's sales cycle / contract problem project you are asking the consultant to perform an assessment of the problem as you see it, make a recommendation to solve it and then, if approved, implement the recommendation.

Decisions around deliverables are not necessarily big enough to warrant use of the Five Languages. The information here is offered to make sure the need is covered and that a **Strategy** or **Execution** conversation happens if needed.

You may need something physical: a report or a presentation of the assessment, what they think it means, and what they recommend based on their observations. Deliverables inform, they're going to be around for a while, and you can work from them as well as refer to them in the future.

Deliverables come in many shapes and sizes. Besides a written report, you may get a strategic plan, research results, a piece of software, staffing or financial models, printed materials, a logo, almost anything defined in the scope of work. Deliverables are set typically by the RFP. However, it could be the consultant comes back in the response and suggests an alternate or additional deliverable. In the end, that decision will be by mutual agreement based on what is needed.

In outlining deliverables, it's less important to dictate number of pages or format than it is to say what it needs to contain. Recall the section on dictating *how* rather than *what*? Think about this: if it's a report, you're going to want to know what the consultant looked at.

Additionally, the best outcome is that the consultant poses the recommendations in the language or languages that best fit the people that need to weigh in on what happens to the recommendations.

For example, if you're trying to solve a problem, what was the problem and what did you look at? How did you approach it? Who did you talk to about the problem? If they make recommendations, what are they based on? What are some other risks and challenges? What options do you have?

If you're looking for a financial model, the deliverable is the model and an explanation of why this model, what was it based on? Who did you to talk to? How do we get from where we are today to that model? How does it fit with the company's vision? What risk is there in using it?

Outlining the deliverables may feel like a checklist of all the things the project should result in at the end. It can be. However, there may be interim deliverables you want as well. During the project, you may need regular status reports from them which are used to keep the project team informed.

Deliverables fall into simple categories:
- Status reports
- Presentations
- Plans
- Training information
- Physical/virtual products (e.g., a piece of furniture or software)
- User manuals/guidelines

It is rare that a project doesn't have a deliverable – when a project has an outcome, more than likely it has a deliverable with it.

Recapping, remember the RFx process is extremely flexible, working with how much time you have, what you find in your research on consultants to do the work needed, and what tools you have for the process (schedules, scorecards, deliverables lists, to name a few). Developing and asking for assumptions helps to define how people think and serves as a basis to have conversations around change or issues.

Recall that schedules apply to both the RFx process as well as the project, deliverables are the knowledge transfer you are "buying" from the consultant and assumptions help everyone understand the basis of pricing and staffing as well as schedule.

Along with all the information desired from the consultant, the Five Languages support the conversations around assumptions made, what the deliverables will be and what the schedule is to complete the RFP and the work. Since all that has been figured out it is time to finish the RFP to find consultants.

Chapter 6 - The Rest of the RFP Process

Project Questions

What has already been done?

What needs to be done?

What decisions have been made?

What decisions will be needed?

Challenges to decision making?

Languages needed?

Great progress has been made: identification of a problem and initiation of a project. Decisions were made to use an internal PM supplemented by external consultants, and to hire those consultants through an RFP process. The Desk project team developed a scope of work and a problem statement, along with deciding to use a formal RFP process to hire the consultant and set the budget.

The discussions have given you an opportunity to learn more about how the stakeholders make decisions through the languages of **Strategy**, **Finance** and **Execution**. The RFP questions selected will provide an opportunity for the consultants to learn how Desk makes decisions (and for future reference, for you to determine if the consultant has a grasp on the Five Languages).

Now what?

- Develop the remainder of the RFP outlining the rules of engagement for the actual process
- Decide what questions will and won't be asked of the consultant
- Determine risk mitigation for competitive intelligence
- Agree on the contract to be used for the consultant
- Decide on and develop evaluation criteria for the proposals and scoring methods
- Decide if consultant interviews will be required
- Determine the final schedule of the RFP process
- Evaluate the proposals
- Determine the short list of consultants, and interview if needed
- Get the budget approval decision and notify the consultant

The challenges to these decisions are usually related to understanding the risks of using or not using the following additions to the RFP.

Communication with the Consultant

No matter how well someone writes an RFP, there are almost always questions from the receiver. A best practice is to limit the point of contact for any questions on the RFP to one person. One point of contact ensures that information going to any responders is consistent and recorded. Imagine the kind of answers you might get if the responders can talk to anyone in the company – it would be chaos and the consultants would most likely be very confused.

At this point, the project team will need to have a discussion on the way to approach questions from consultants. You will most likely use the language of **Strategy**, focusing on what you need to accomplish and how much information you are willing to give out.

Considered in this discussion are: What is the method by which they will ask and you will answer? Who answers what type of questions? Who has the authority to answer contract questions? What is the risk that questions will be answered by someone who doesn't know the correct answer?

One very common decision is if it would be helpful to have a group meeting or phone call with all the consultants the RFP has gone to. From an RFP issuer's point of view, this seems the simplest to manage. From a consultant's point of view, this kind of session is not always useful as there is a chance their firm might ask a question another firm hadn't thought of thereby revealing a competitive advantage or insight to the approach.

One way to mitigate this issue is to hold separate question and answer sessions. There has to be agreement on how deep in the details Desk is willing to go before holding the session. Then, the team can take the recorded questions and answers and combine them into a single document, which they send out to the full group of consultants.

The second method is more time consuming, so it may take a conversation in the language of **Execution** both while deciding on this approach and when deciding the overall process schedule. This conversation will cover the risks of each approach and how much longer the schedule will be if there are separate question and answer sessions. Recall that there is some urgency from Desk's management team to get the consultant in and resolve the contract issue so the CEO's growth vision can get back on track.

Getting a Sense of the Consultants – The Questions

This is probably one of the hardest sections for an RFP team to put together. There are a myriad of decisions on what to ask and how to ask it so you can get a feel for which of the consultants on your list are the best for the work. The questions need to be designed to see if the consultant speaks the Five Languages and can clearly communicate their thought processes.

Standard, tactical questions about the consultant's business were covered in Chapter 5. The questions in this section are more pointed toward how they will do or approach the work rather than about their company specifically. Some of the best questions of this type are based in managing the schedule, budget, changes to the scope of work, and personnel.

Schedule questions might focus on how the consultant manages the timeline, what they do when they are behind or ahead, and examples of how they have prevented issues in past projects. Personnel questions might focus on what a consultant would do if a key member of their team decides to leave. Budget management and scope change questions could ask about their approach to communicating or managing cost issues (which can affect the schedule, quality of project results, and deliverables).

The RFP team's conversations will focus on the decisions that drive the use of the Five Languages by the consultant. In addition, they will give the consultant opportunities to discover what is important to you. If you think in terms of Vision, **Finance**, **Execution**, **Change**, and **Strategy**, questions may show themselves naturally.

Think of it this way: if you ask a budget management question, it can be situational. For example, "What do you provide to clients when a change in the scope of work is needed?" or, "How do you help clients make critical decisions?" This leaves room for the consultant to show you what language they know (or not), as well as how they approach decision conversations.

Competitive Intelligence Management

In the RFP process it is very important to have conversations about risk, and how to manage confidential information in an RFP. Possibly, the problem that is to be solved can impact the competitive advantage of your company. The outline of the situation may contain competitive intelligence. Therefore, the decision will be on how much information to release and how to control the dissemination of that information.

Remembering that consultants may work all over any market, they may also work or have worked for your competition. You will want to have some form of mitigation for both the RFP information and the results they come up with.

In this situation, companies will typically require consultants to sign a Non-Disclosure Agreement (NDA) before receiving any RFx, and it is a good practice to do so. The primary decision makers on the Desk project will need to agree on the level of risk they are willing tolerate. The structure of the RFP information will need to meet that risk level through careful wording as well as an NDA, should it be decided to use one.

Amendment Process

Sometimes during the RFP process more information becomes available after the original RFP has been released to consultants. A typical approach to this is to issue an amendment updating the responding consultants with the new information. At times it may also be necessary to change the timeline of the RFP itself – an amendment is used for that as well. The original RFP should describe how amendments will be issued and who will issue them so the consultants know it is an official amendment.

The language of **Strategy** can be used for the approach to amendments. In the case of the Desk project, it may be that the scope of work is relatively simple and no additional information would be relevant to the consultants. Many times, if there is a question and answer period for the consultants, answers to specific questions may drive a change in the scope of work, schedule, or other parts of the project. Then an amendment might be issued.

An amendment may also lead to other decisions about schedule. Recall that Desk management is eager to get this project underway. The languages of **Execution** and **Finance** may need to come into play when discussing the options and consequences (especially risk) to issuing an amendment or not.

Contract and Negotiation

If the company has an up-to-date consultant contract, it is advisable to include it in the RFP and ask consultants for any objections they might have to any parts of the contract. Typical contract clauses consultants try to negotiate are payment clauses, insurance requirements, and Intellectual Property (IP) ownership. There is more detail on all of these in Chapter 7. A best practice is to note in the RFP which clauses are non-negotiable so the consultant can decide if the contract is something they wish to work with.

The language of **Finance**, which covers financial issues and risk, will be used to get agreement on which clauses in the contract are non-negotiable. The language of **Finance** helps the CFO understand the potential trade-off between negotiating any of the clauses and holding firm. Incorporating the language of **Strategy** will lay out the plan for negotiations, and where firm line is in those negotiations.

From the consultant side, understanding the non-negotiable portions of the contract gives them a very clear view of what is important to the company and what the company will flex on. It allows them to have their own internal discussions in the language of **Finance** on the risk of accepting the terms.

Evaluation Criteria

Every consultant will want to know the evaluation criteria as this helps them understand what to emphasize in their proposal. Again, it also helps them understand what is important to you and gives an extra view into how you make decisions.

Some of the more common criteria are:

- Completeness and clarity of the proposal: was everything answered, were all deliverables provided, is the consultant's train of thought clear
- Staff and company qualifications
- Relevant experience with the scope of work
- Familiarity with your company
- Approach and thought processes in responses
- Costs of the services

Not all of the above will apply to any given RFP, and it is also not an exhaustive list. The evaluation criteria will depend on what you are asking for.

Choosing evaluation criteria will require conversations in the languages of **Strategy** and **Finance**.

Perhaps the standard in your company is to take the lowest price, no matter what. Having a conversation about not automatically taking the lowest price will center on the value of what a more expensive consultant brings versus the lowest cost.

Additionally, any plans for cost options, savings, or value increase will need to be reviewed and related back to the originally discussed ROI of solving the sales cycle problem expediently. This is a critical, make-or-break conversation impacting the choice of the consultant in the future.

What They Learn About You

After all the conversations about the parts to be included in the RFP, it will be put together and sent out to the consultants. How the RFP is written and the information included in the RFP as a result of all the decisions made will give consultants a lot of information about you, how you will treat them, and how you make decisions.

It is close to impossible to communicate everything in a way that sets as impartial and unbiased a stage for every consultant preparing to respond to an RFP. The decisions made on each item included in the RFP do need to have a component of respect for the consultant, even in the midst of any sense of urgency.

Desk's management finds itself at a critical point with solving the sales contract problem and may feel pressured to shorten project durations or cut corners to get the work done faster. In the languages of **Strategy** or **Execution**, the options and consequences of moving too fast must include the toll taken on the consultants themselves.

As a consultant, I had the job of both writing and issuing RFPs for other consultants to answer, as well as writing proposals to answer RFPs from clients. Once, I had a client with a very complicated project that had taken a long time to get approved. My job was to write and issue the RFP for the project's general contractor. The client wanted the RFP released on December 5th and responses back on January 2nd.

Consider the proposal response time: 26 days spanning two very significant holidays! (The math isn't wrong, it takes a day to issue and a day to submit, even in the best timelines.) Given that the client typically wasn't available from December 15 – 31, and the responders had vacation plans for a good portion of the response period, this was an RFP that was fraught with risk to the client.

The highest risk was getting no or low-quality responses: it seemed an unreasonable ask by the client and an impossible task by the responders. There were many conversations that followed involving the Five Languages. Among them were the client's ability to support the RFP at the time of year, the risk of no response or low quality responses, or the cost of possibly having to do the RFP over again when the holidays were over.

As an RFP issuer, approaches like this can certainly lead to market perceptions that you don't respect those you want to have work for you.

Consultants learn about you in the timeline of the RFP process itself. The timeline is critical in keeping things moving, and it can also serve as a test of how well the consultant can respond under deadline conditions. Perhaps there have been a lot of amendments to the RFP (this may happen a lot in public entity bid situations), and the due date changes.

If you feel you have given ample time for responses, but a consultant comes back and asks for more time, they are probably not a consultant you want. A request for more time may indicate how that consultant might meet deadlines in the work. Holding a hard line on due dates sends a message to consultants that your dates mean your dates.

After Proposals are Back

During RFP development you had many conversations in the Five Languages about the approach to the RFP and what information was included in it. Evaluation criteria was developed and agreed upon. Decisions were made about contract negotiation points. You have sent the RFP to the consultants and now the proposals are back. What's next?

A lot of tactical activities were completed during the time the consultants were writing their proposals. And, some of the activities got the RFP team familiar with the tools they will use in the evaluation and how the process will work.

A key tool in the proposal evaluation phase is the evaluation matrix. The evaluation matrix is the ranking tool and the record of how your consultant selection was made. Therefore, your proposal team must understand what the evaluation criteria are and how to interpret them, numerical ranking scale, the weight (relative importance) of each criterion, as well as what they will be evaluating.

Evaluating the Responses

Reviewing the evaluation matrix is an optimal time to examine the decisions made while developing the RFP so the entire team is on the same page and understands how and why the consultants will be evaluated.

Recall that the strategy is to have an external consultant assess perceived contract negotiation issues that cause Desk's long sales cycle. The RFP has been issued to help select a consultant who can assess the situation and issues, develop a solution (and an approach to implement it), with an option to complete the implementation if the company agrees.

For the project team, in the language of **Strategy**, a review of the RFP and project plan helps connect both the solving of the problem and how that solution supports the CEO's vision for company growth. Using the language of **Finance**, reconfirm that the RFP results will set the budget for the project and outline the decisions made about insurance, payment terms, IP ownership, and all the other RFP requirements. **Execution** language supports the review of how the team will work together, what resources were agreed upon, and what the team has approval to do.

For the evaluation of the consultants' proposals, you and the project team will have to agree on what the most important measures of skills, abilities and experience are. In addition, you will need to determine what the relative weight of each measure is.

For example, it is extremely difficult to measure the quality of the consultant's thought process, but it is something you might want to look for. An evaluation measure might be the consultant's ability to clearly communicate their thought process (and, this could be more important than if they completed each part of the proposal in full).

Actual story: I ran a complicated RFP process for a client, with five responders. Reading the first three proposals was one of the most painful processes I had gone through in a long time – there was a ton of marketing information in them without much substance. Reading this kind of proposal is a lot like going on a scavenger hunt without a list. You look around for the nugget and never find it.

By the fourth proposal I hated my life...and then it happened. A breath of fresh air in the form of some straightforward answers, clearly articulated answers to questions, and requirements that showed train of thought. They also included statements around how their expertise matched the need the client had in terms of the Five Languages.

They had actually figured out from the RFP document how the client thought and made decisions. Unfortunately, they skipped a portion of the RFP (I think by accident). However, the unanimous decision was made to allow them to go forward because the rest of the proposal was so good. We elected to cover the missed section of the proposal in an interview. The weight of the measure of clear thinking was much higher than the weight of completing all the sections. The decision was made using the language of **Vision**, what was the overall vision for the success of the RFP. Keeping the additional consultant kept with that vision.

I wouldn't recommend this as a standard approach – the higher weight was rigorously discussed and voted on both before the proposals came in and when the team elected to get the missing information in an interview.

The evaluation matrix is pivotal in the RFP process as it is the basis of how you made your consultant selection. While it is important to make sure the project team understands what is important to the hiring decision, you have to translate that matrix into a language that will resonate with the reviewers and make it easy for them to rate the responses. Remember, the Five Languages aren't just for the C-Suite or decision makers, everyone uses/hears in some form of those languages.

Now, it's time to look at the aggregated evaluation scores and decide if interviews are in order.

To Interview or Not to Interview

Aggregating the evaluation scores is fairly straight-forward to complete. Evaluation matrices developed in an electronic spreadsheet program can do most of the work for the team once they enter their information. The decision to hire can be complicated if rankings are close. The interview process helps differentiate consultants who might be closely scored after all the proposals are read.

Consider that you started the RFP process of the sales cycle / contract negotiation project with a list of five possible consultants. The RFP team's evaluations have helped pare the list down to three, and all of them have scored within a close range of each other, making it difficult to come to a clear decision. This is where interviewing can help.

The consultant's proposals contained their qualifications and other information pertinent to your decision to hire them. The response may have generated questions about how they think, their qualifications, experience, expertise, project approach, staffing, schedule, or price.

The interview is the place to really learn about them, their team, how they will interact with you, and the other project team members at Desk. It will also give them an opportunity to showcase their knowledge of the Five Languages. Interviews are optional, but highly recommended.

Developing interview questions is very specific to the individual responses. Interviews help form a good understanding of the team, any critical components that need clarification, an opportunity for more situational questions, and gauge the consultant's ability to deal with curveballs.

A best practice for the interview team as they review proposals is to jot notes while reading. This captures clarifications and deeper explanations needed, or verifications of something that might appear to have been missed. The more difficult matter is how to develop questions that will elicit answers in the Five Languages.

You may want to know more about how the consultant plans to confirm the problem – who they will talk to so they can understand the issue (and why those particular people). This will require the consultant to show their knowledge of the language of **Vision** – why it is a problem and what happens if nothing is done. Perhaps it is important to know how they will develop a solution. What will they be sensitive to? Do they bring the language of **Change** into the mix? Why the change? What's in it for the employees?

Once there is a discussion of **Change**, you might want to structure a question so they need to answer in the languages of **Strategy** and **Execution** – what the plan is and why that particular approach. Approach questions will certainly start to reveal their knowledge of the language of **Finance** as well; including cost, cost risk, time value of money, etc.

An interesting approach in interviews is to rotate the questions through each of the interviewers. This allows questions to be asked in different ways, and for the interviewers to listen for any of the Five Languages in the answers. However, if someone is uncomfortable with asking a question that may be outside of their expertise, it is simple enough to change the order of the questions. The RFP team should go through the questions and prioritize them. That way, if time runs short in the interview because of a long discussion, the most important ones will be the first asked.

Interviews are critical to get a sense of what the consultants are really like and how they will interact with you. How the consultants communicate with you in the interview will give a sense of how well they can learn your company's culture of decision making and use the Five Languages with you.

Interviews are also a great place to gauge the consultant's listening skills. Everyone gets nervous in an interview – even the most experienced – and I've heard some pretty entertaining answers to questions I haven't asked!

Given that you are bringing a consultant in to assess a business problem, most of what they need to do is listen. If their listening skills are low, they're not going to hear the subtleties of the things they assess and connect ideas. It is absolutely acceptable to stop them and restate the question if it seems like the answer has nothing to do with what you asked.

One mistake consultants often make is to assume one client thinks like the next and has the same culture of decision making. If you get a sense during the interview they were not listening for clues about you or were making assumptions for their answers based on another client, pay attention.

Sometimes consultants spend so much time with one client they start to believe everyone talks and thinks like that one client. Don't get me wrong, there is something to learn of the Five Languages with every client. To have a consultant that understands the Five Languages, but applies them as if they were talking to someone else can be a bit frustrating.

What happens if the interview goes horribly wrong? There certainly are instances the proposal was excellent, every box was checked, and yet...the interview is horrible. I have had an occasion where I realized I could not work with the consultant in front of me. Their proposal was well written, they had great qualifications, but the team in the room was arrogant and un-coachable (important in a consultant). I felt like they thought they were doing me a favor and I was pretty sure I was going to get data, not information, to make decisions with. This was not a good choice for the company.

One of the most common issues in an interview is one person in the room talking too much – and it's not the one you're going to be working with. This is a great place to see if knowledge of the Five Languages permeates the consultant's entire organization. The interview is the opportunity to see how the consultant's representative (who actually does the work) will deal with you.

It is also a time to see if they can learn how you operate, think like you, and speak the Five Languages to you as needed. A way to deal with the over talker is to decide who is most important to have in the interviews and indicate that only those people can attend. This also lets you find out if the consultant's representative has the authority to do the work and make decisions on behalf of their company.

Situations like the above are why robust conversations with the RFP team are critical to have. These conversations with the team bring out what is important to them to know about the consultant, what they are listening for in the interview, and how to approach questions to see best sense if the consultant will be able to figure you out.

Interview Structure

One of the decisions to guide the RFP team through is the length, structure, and management of the interview itself. The content, format, and length of an interview will be based on what you are trying to get out of it. The more complicated or expensive the project is, the longer the interview tends to be. Sometimes interviews are designed as working sessions with a goal to see a live example of how the consultant approaches their work, runs a workshop, or interviews people.

Interviews need to run on time, both during the interview and between consecutive interviews. An upfront strategy discussion will help with the decision of how long the interview will be, and how to keep it moving if it bogs down. If the consultant answers all the questions before time is up, consider going back to previous questions and asking them from a different context. This can give you a better sense of how they will help you make decisions, communicate information, or go about their work. The Five Languages will, hopefully, show up in the continued conversation.

Leaving time between interviews allows for breakdown of technology, passing out cards, having a quick conversation, requesting additional information, or taking a break. It also allows time for the proposal team to talk together about what they heard, if anything was missed, or if they were confused by anything. No decisions will get made right there, although clarifications could be gathered for follow up with the consultant if needed.

Interview Results

Once the interviews are done, the process of gathering feedback from the RFP team will be repeated and added to the results from the proposal reviews. Once that work is done, it's time to make a decision on who to hire.

Short Listing

This overall process can seem like a lot of work – especially when it is just to hire a consultant. Of course, the first consultant talked to can be hired if you can successfully manage the risks of getting a consultant without the right qualifications or at the right price in the time you need it done. Regardless, the RFP process gives the greatest opportunity for an objective hire.

Recall that there were five proposal responses for Desk's project. After the preliminary evaluations that group was narrowed down to three for interviews. Your interviews are done, the scores have been collated, and the summary comparison matrix developed. The comparison matrix shows ranking of each consultant after proposal submission, after interviews, and review of pricing. If contract comments were allowed during the RFP process, any negotiating points should be in the comparison matrix.

All three consultants were close in ranking after interviews. Recall that earlier, during RFP development, the decision was made with the CFO not to automatically take the lowest priced consultant. Because the consultants are all close in ranking other considerations need to be taken into account such as:

- Qualifications and experience compared to each other
- Personality fit with the company
- Clear train of thought and knowledge of the Five Languages (if any)
- Contract negotiation points
- Pricing

You are facing a decision point. To keep things simple for this particular consultant selection, there are a couple of items that might be deciding factors: price and contract negotiation points. For this example, assume two of the consultants (Consultants A and B) have very similar pricing while the third (Consultant C) is about double the price of either of the other two. It also happens that Consultant C has taken issue with some contract terms, which cannot be negotiated the way they want them. Therefore, Consultant C can be placed last on the selection list.

As you discuss the final two with your proposal team you can start developing the justification for hiring your number one pick. From the conversations with the CFO and COO throughout the RFP process, you have picked up the language they speak and the things that are specifically important to them.

The evaluation and summary comparison matrices will be the basis of your conversation in the languages of **Finance**, **Execution** and **Strategy**. You can practice this conversation with the team as you decide which consultant to pick.

Remind the team of the business reasons for the RFP in the first place: a long sales cycle leading to lower revenue recognition which in turn slows the growth of the company. And, remember the goal of the RFP is to hire a consultant to assess/confirm the perceived problem of contract issues and recommend a solution for solving the problem. Also, recall the risk of not solving the problem, how the project will be executed, and the results of the RFP process. In the end, because of pricing, overall fit, and contract terms acceptance, you and the team agree that Consultant B is your first choice.

Best practice for the results of an RFP process is to keep the evaluation and summary comparison matrices, a copy of the RFP and proposals from each consultant, interview questions and a list of the proposal team members as a record of the decision.

The matrices are the basis for your hiring justification. The other information can be used to take other stakeholders through the hiring process. All of this information is an inventory of the proposal team's insights on each firm and how they thought the consultants stacked up against the RFP requirements.

Communicating the Results to the Consultants

Consultant B has been identified as the best hire for the project, based on the RFP process. A sound approach to notifying the consultants is to contact your first choice first and make sure they are ready, available, and willing to take the work. Confirming this is important: it is possible that Consultant B has accepted other work while you were making your decision. Once you confirm with Consultant B, then move on to Consultants A and C and advise them of your choice.

Remember that approval of the budget for the project is still outstanding. Therefore, you will need to advise Consultant B of the activities you need to complete before they can actually start the work. Another opportunity to help them understand how decisions are made at Desk!

Full download from the entire process for both winning and losing consultants is essential and should be built into the process. It is extremely frustrating for a consultant to get passed over for a job and not know how to get better. It's also good for a consultant to know why they were chosen so they keep doing things that lead to their success.

Budget Approval

Part of the goal of the RFP process was to set the project budget. Early conversations with the CFO, CEO and COO helped with problem identification and RFP development. Those conversations covered the impacts of the problem to the company **Vision**, the **Finance** implications of not solving the problem and the estimated internal cost, as well as the possible ROI of the project and resources needed to execute the project.

Results from the RFP process include the evaluation matrices, each of the consultant's proposals, interview questions and notes, and the summary comparison matrix developed to make the final decision. The comparison matrix is the tool that will support your first budget approval conversation with the CFO. In some companies, the procurement department is the first conversation. However, in this case the RFP team is acting as procurement and is aware that the budget for the project will be set by the RFP process.

A comparison matrix shows all the consultants, their ranking in both the proposal and interview evaluations, their proposed price, any contract terms they wish to negotiate, and their qualifications or expertise relating to the project. Any other evaluation criteria information can be added. The matrix will be unique to the RFP and can contain anything that is pertinent to the budget or hiring decision.

The CFO will be interested in some specific information and the language of **Finance** will be your tool to communicate with him. The information includes:

- The estimated cost of the project showing both consultant and internal resource costs (if any).
- Any financial impacts of the existing problem (if known). Note that part of the problem identification could have included a financial analysis of the impacts of the long sales cycle.
- Any anticipated costs over the base estimated cost of the project. It could be that the consultant offered some cost savings options in their approach. Those need to be taken into account.
- Estimated cost of the implementation based on the consultant's approach. Because the results of the assessment are still unknown, implementation of a project to fix the problem was not part of the RFP. You may have asked the consultant to estimate that, based on their assessment/recommendation approach.
- Contract terms to be negotiated, if any.
- Cash flow projection for the project.
- Project plan/schedule and any risks of delay.
- Any contingency[8] you might need. There are mixed approaches to contingency. Bottom line, the consultant doesn't get to know what your contingency is, if you have one. Some CFOs prefer to approve the cost of the project without contingency so funds that may or may not be

---

[8] Contingency is funds in your budget to deal with unexpected things encountered during the work or to address added scope. Not an amount typically shared with the consultant. It may or may not be a practice at your company to have a contingency.

spent remain available to the company. If there is a need for additional funds on a project, this approach also maintains the need to have another **Finance** conversation.

In your conversation with the CFO, you will need to articulate the basis of the team's decision and why the choice was for a consultant other than the lowest cost, if that is the case. Additionally, covering the summary comparison matrix to show the value of services provided versus the cost. A value conversation can be hard – the CFO may look at value differently than a project manager.

In the case of the consultant hire, value might be the advantages consultant B brings over the others compared to the relative cost. By way of simple example, if Consultant B has more specific experience in the kind of problem to be solved, they have higher value for their cost than another consultant whose cost is roughly the same, but who does not have the same experience.

You will also need to show the CFO that you understand the impacts of the financial decision you are asking him to make. You have a financial impact analysis of the problem, and you know the cost of the project, so you can start to have an ROI discussion.

It helps to bring the company's revenue-to-spend ratio[9] in this conversation. This simple ratio is a great way to really understand what it takes to spend money on the project, and lets the CFO know you are a serious steward of the company's assets.

Since Consultant B accepts all contract terms, little discussion on contracting risk will be needed with the CFO. However, a review of any changes to standard clauses made at RFP development would be helpful at time of budget approval.

The cash flow discussion will work its way into the discussion as you look at the schedule with the CFO. If there are any considerations to cash flow, now is the time to ask the CFO in order to adjust the schedule accordingly.

A scenario might be the company is in the process of making large capital investments, and if your cash flow projects a payment to your consultant at the same time as another large outlay of cash. The CFO is reluctant to use the company's line of credit to manage this situation. The project schedule may have to be adjusted to smooth out cash flow.

---

[9] Revenue to spend ratio: a calculation of the amount of revenue the company needs to generate to have a dollar to spend. The CFO can help calculate that number

In the language of **Strategy**, the project plan shows where you are going from here, the internal resources needed, how long it will take, and when the company might start to see the benefits of the change in the sales cycle length.

Next comes a conversation with the COO. You have had conversations during the RFP development and execution process that set the stage for final approval. As with the CFO, a review of the problem identification and the decision to hire an outside consultant set the stage. Having all your RFP results with you is advisable.

In terms of the language of **Execution**, the COO will want to know how long the project will take and who of her resources you need to use to get it done. Engaging the COO on strategic use of internal resources may also result in some innovative and cost effective approaches to using those resources.

Because the results of the assessment are not yet known, the budget approval conversation will probably not reveal any operational efficiencies as a result of the project. However, the conversation is a place to listen for what the COO is thinking about or hoping for when the sales cycle problem is solved. You can then take those thoughts and work with your consultant during the project to see if the recommended solution addresses them.

Once you have gotten approval from the CFO and COO, you may move on to the CEO. If direct communication with the CEO is not part of your company's process, you have more than provided the information the COO and CFO need to get approval from the CEO.

In the language of **Vision**, the problem identification covered the impact of the sales cycle problem to realizing the company's goals. The project is the first step to confirming the problem and finding the solution. Finding the solution will allow the CEO to refocus energy on leading and evangelizing the company, and fulfilling the business vision.

Successful use of the languages of **Vision**, **Finance**, **Execution**, and **Strategy** have garnered an approval of the budget for the sales cycle / contract problem project. Using an RFx process you have learned how the CEO, COO and CFO think about financial and execution decisions and business risks. You have articulated the information they need in their language.

Although RFxs are a straightforward process, they can take a lot of time. Summarizing the ideas above, this process needs to include the rules of engagement, take care of making sure competitive intelligence isn't shared, and involve a key set of people to help make the selection. Educating the team on the tools (evaluation matrices, scoring methods, and questions) is essential and a great use of time while the consultants are working on their proposals.

Communicating how the decision will be made in the languages of the CFO, COO and CEO will help your team improve their skills with the languages. The budget approval decision will be about communicating the proposal team's choice and why, based on all you have learned from the beginning and your use of the Five Languages.

Chapter 7 - Contracting[10]

Project Questions

What has already been done?

What needs to be done?

What decisions have been made?

What decisions will be needed?

Challenges to decision making?

Languages needed?

All right, a lot has been done so far! It probably seems like getting through the RFP has taken a while. The good news is, the more the Five Languages are practiced and used, the faster decisions can be made. There is no guarantee, of course. Decision-making conversations can be drawn out because of availability of the people to participate in them, the need to filter data down to information, and the development of the key points of the conversation in the language they need to be in.

If you are trying to determine if your project has been taking too long, a good rule for the timing of all that has happened in the preceding chapters is a couple of months.

---

[10] No information in this chapter should be construed as legal advice. Consult in-house or outside legal counsel before negotiating any contract or changing a standing contract in any way.

Getting to the decision to hire a consultant could take about a month and going through the RFP process (if you are really moving) is another month. This is good information to have when you kick off the effort, as someone will surely ask. And recall that Desk is in a hurry because the problem is coming to a head and starting to interfere with the CEO's vision for company growth.

So far, Desk has determined they really do have a sales contracting problem they would like to solve. You have been chosen as the internal project manager and you led the decision conversations to hire an outside consultant due to resource constraints (using the languages of **Execution** and **Strategy**).

The project team was formed and it was determined with the COO that an RFP process would be used. This decision was discussed in the languages of **Strategy** and **Vision**. Recall that Desk's COO has a vision for a procurement group and sees this RFP process as a way to determine the resources needed to form it.

You have led the project team in developing the RFP and along the way have used the languages of **Execution**, **Strategy** and **Finance** to set the direction for the RFP, as well as use the process to determine the project budget. The project team has evaluated responses and interviews based on what is important to Desk in the consultant they hire. The budget from the RFP has been approved by the CFO and COO based on conversations in the languages of **Vision**, **Strategy** and **Execution**.

The consultant has been chosen, and it is time to put a contract in place so they can do the work. Most of the decisions about a contract involve risk – risk to Desk versus risk to the consultant. Going forward, contract decision conversations may involve the following questions:

- Does your company have a consultant contract?
- If not, is the company willing to sign the consultant's?
- Who will negotiate the contract on behalf of Desk?
- How and when will you pay the consultant?
- What insurance will you require?
- How will changes to the contract be handled?
- What discussions about intellectual property protections are needed?
- Are any other contract clauses needed?

Some of the challenges to getting these decisions made may rest on the experience of the company with hiring consultants. If Desk doesn't hire consultants often, the decisions may take a little longer because of lack of familiarity.

However, Desk does have a legal department who deals with contracts all the time – they might be a great source of information and assistance. As stated in the footnote at the beginning of this chapter, all that follows are things to think about and are not to be construed as legal advice – all final decisions should be made with advice from legal counsel.

Your Contract or Theirs

Many companies don't hire consultants very often and as a result they may not have a consultant contract form to use. In Desk's case, because a procurement department will be formed in the near future it might be time to develop an in-house contract. Discussions with the COO in the languages of **Strategy** and **Execution** might include weighing the options of the time to develop a contract versus using the consultant's contract as a basis for future contracts.

Remember that the CEO has placed some urgency around getting the sales contract/cycle length issue solved as soon as possible. The big question will be, "Can we get the contract completed in a timeframe that supports the issue being solved quickly?" That answer, ultimately, is "No" (based on weighing the impact to the timeline of solving the problem caused by waiting for a contract to be developed).

Desk's project team, including the COO and CFO, choose to use the consultant's contract for the project. The risk in this case is that the terms and conditions of a consultant contract will usually be written in favor of the consultant. That is, their contract will move risk to the client (Desk) and create more favorable terms for payment, termination, delays, and changes. Most consultant contracts concentrate on quick payment, minimal expenditures for insurance, and ownership of all the things created while working for you (e.g., intellectual property).

By way of example, perhaps the consultant's scope of work included producing a manual or procedure document for you. The way their contract is structured they most likely "own" what they created for you, which means you may only use it with their express permission.

Permission is most likely included in the contract, however, I have seen occasions where the client gets to use what was created and the consultant is the only one that can alter it. The end result is the consultant controls their output and you have to pay to have your manual or procedure documentation altered.

The decision to use the consultant's contract included discussions in the language of **Finance** about payment terms and insurance. Payment terms affect cash flow and budget, insurance terms outline the risk (and cost) to Desk based on coverage required. In the language of **Execution**, the discussions will be centered on how to deal with the need to change something in the future, and what work the consultant will own, or not (see the section later in this chapter on Intellectual Property ownership).

Negotiation

I've found contract negotiation can be a touchy subject – contract terms can be interpreted in many ways, depending on how clearly the contract is written. The discussions around contract negotiations will be primarily based in the languages of **Finance** and **Execution**, with a little **Strategy** thrown in. Given that consultants will usually want to negotiate payment terms (time to pay, discounts), insurance types and amounts, termination clauses and IP ownership, the COO and CFO will certainly be involved in the negotiations in some form.

Procurement typically negotiates contracts, in partnership with a legal department, if you have both. Given that Desk does not yet have a procurement group, there may be contract specialist in legal. Recall you have had a representative from the legal group on the team from the get-go. They have been involved in all the discussions about RFP information, decisions about changes to contract terms based on discussions with the stakeholders, the strategy of the RFP process, as well as solving the problem itself and communication of the RFP and project schedule. All of these discussions have been primarily based in the languages of **Finance**, **Execution** and **Strategy**.

Lacking a procurement group or contract specialist, the negotiator would typically be the PM. There is an approach that works pretty well for smoothing out the process. The PM is given the authority to negotiate, but does not have the authority to finalize, by being educated in what the company will allow or will tolerate as terms and which terms are not to be touched.

The PM negotiates in this manner, and then gets final approval from the person with the appropriate level of authority. Working with this approach is a fabulous place to understand what the company wants in the way of protections, their tolerance for risk, how the specific contract fits in with the larger portfolio of contracts, what is important in a contracting situation, and how contractual relationships are viewed.

Payment Terms

In the language of **Finance**, alteration of payment terms deals with cash flow impact to the company as well as the consultant. Strategically, companies like to keep cash flow as steady as possible and avoid spikes. For example, additional cash demand when the company is in the process of making big capital investments can be hazardous to the company's financial health. A conversation with the CFO can help you understand the overall company financial forecast and cash flow strategy as you negotiate payment terms.

There are some strategies companies employ in contracts that help protect cash flow or make cash flow more predictable:

1. **Payment in a certain timeframe:** the consultant submits and invoice and the company then has a defined length of time to pay. Typical time frames are 30, 60 or 90 days. Sixty-day pay is a relatively standard time frame. Smaller consultants will want to reduce this to 30 days, or shorter, if they can get it. The payment time frame affects the consultant's cash flow as well - you can see where they might be having a discussion on this internally in the language of **Finance**.

2. **Quick pay with discount:** The consultant gets
    paid in a shorter time frame (10 or 15 days) and
    the company takes a discount for the reduction
    in payment cycle time. Many consultants might
    be willing to take the discount to have a more
    predictable cash flow. In this case, a conversa-
    tion with the CFO, in the language of **Finance**,
    about cash flow is highly recommended as a
    quick pay can cause some havoc when cash is
    tight. Recall that Desk is having issues with rev-
    enue delays (cash flow) because of the sales con-
    tract length.

Insurance Requirements

Another commonly negotiated requirement is insurance types and amounts (or coverage). Decisions on insurance types and requirements will
take place in the language of **Finance**, given the
CFO is usually highly interested in financial risk,
which is what insurance is all about.

The most common types of insurance required of
consultants are Commercial General Liability (pro-
tects a business owner from claims of negligence related to business activities among other things),
Automobile and perhaps Errors and Omissions

(E&O, also known as professional liability[11]) insurance. Some companies may also require specific Theft insurance.

As outlined in Chapter 5, insurance requirements may vary from one consultant to another. To keep with that example, if a consultant is going to work remotely and never step foot in your office, then Theft insurance may not be a reasonable requirement of the consultant. A conversation with the COO or CFO about this kind of risk would be helpful so you can understand how they might make the decision on Theft insurance.

The consultant will expect a requirement for the more common types of insurance. The negotiation point will be the amount of insurance required. The consultant's contract may carry a certain amount of coverage reasonable for the type of work they do and the risks involved.

Your company may require a higher amount than the consultant regularly carries. This is a decision point or negotiation – the consultant can refuse to increase insurance because of the increased premium cost. You can also negotiate to pay all or a

---

[11] E&O Insurance is typically, but not always, limited to architects and engineers where an error or omission in their work might result in great injury, harm or financial loss.

portion of the increased premium for the duration of your project.

Before you enter into this kind of negotiation, have a conversation with the CFO or COO to determine the strategy of insurance coverage for your project.

The scope of work for the sales cycle / contract project is an assessment, recommendation and possible implementation of a problem solution. The implementation may be as simple as a contract and process change. Not a very risky project for either party, particularly since legal is on your project team. A conversation on insurance strategy will help determine what type of insurance to require and at what level.

Termination

Sometimes work doesn't go the way everyone wants it to and a contract has to be terminated. The language of **Strategy** can be used to have a discussion with the project team, CFO and COO about how and when to terminate, if the need arises.

Options for termination are "with cause" and "without cause." Another decision will be whether or not to allow both sides, you and the consultant, to be able to terminate the contract in either "cause" situation.

The option to terminate "without cause" is often reserved only for the contract holder. In the case of the consultant's contract being used the holder would be the consultant, so be careful. No matter who holds the contract, "without cause" allows the holder to terminate the contract for any reason.

A "with cause" option requires a certain event to have occurred such as non-performance, breach of contract, or non-payment (on the contract holder's side). No matter which of the termination situations are chosen, there will typically be a requirement for a notice period of some length.

A way to help the CFO think about which termination clauses to use might be this: both sides get the right to terminate "with cause." This creates a scenario where something specific has to happen in order to terminate the contract. Then, only Desk gets the right to terminate "without cause," giving you the right to terminate as needed.

Consultants will most likely want any termination clauses in the contract to include their right to terminate "without cause" as well. Termination "with cause" by the consultant usually involves non-payment by the contract holder. This is not the only situation, though it is probably the most common.

The consultant will also want the longest notice period possible. Thirty days is typical – a longer notice period gives the consultant more time to shift their personnel to another project and lessen any disruption to their business due to a termination.

Payment at termination is also a negotiation point when a contract holder terminates a consultant. While specific to the conditions resulting in termination, generally if the termination is without cause, the contract will specify payment owed for work completed up to the termination date. If the termination is with cause, the contract will need to specify the conditions of payment based on the cause.

There may be some history to termination clauses in your company's contract, if you have one. In Desk's case, because you have elected to use the consultant's contract, termination clauses will need to be closely examined by legal. In the language of **Finance**, you will also want the CFO to help decide what payment impacts are involved with termination. Any negotiation of termination clauses should be made after a conversation with the appropriate decision makers.

Intellectual Property Ownership

Intellectual property (IP) ownership will be critical to the consultant. In the past, IP usually meant software. This has changed drastically and the trend is for everything to be considered IP. Because this is such a sensitive and tricky issue the best approach is to consult with legal counsel when dealing with IP ownership.

Payment Types or Fee Structures

During the RFP process, one item of discussion may have been around the fee structure you wanted from the consultant. Fee structure dictates how the consultant bases their price for the work. Given the cash flow situation at Desk, you may have had a conversation in the language of **Finance** about the risks of various fee structures and how to control costs. This is of particular interest when you are using the RFP to set the budget.

In talking about the options and consequences with the CFO, it was decided, since there is no rule at this point at Desk, to let the consultant decide the best way to price the work. Consultants will structure fees based on their business model and the nature of the work. There are a few different structures, each has its risks and advantages:

1. **Time and materials (T&M)**

   Also known as hourly rates, this type of fee structure is based on an estimate of time and costs of any materials for a defined scope of work. The generally accepted makeup of hourly rates is wages, indirect costs (rent, utilities, or sales, for example), general and administrative expenses, and profit.

   The risk in this type of fee structure is mostly to the client, unless the contract is not-to-exceed. Not-to-exceed means the consultant has estimated the amount of time to do the work and the costs of materials for the scope of work in the contract and is agreeing not to go over that amount. The only time the not-to-exceed amount would change is if you decide to add or delete scope.

   With T&M, since you don't dictate how the work gets accomplished (recalling the what/how conversation), you are relying on the consultant to have estimated the hours for the work correctly.

   This is the crux of an "estimate." It is just that – an approximate cost for the scope of work to be accomplished the way the consultant thinks it can be done. The risk to you is if the consultant runs into a problem with completing the work, you will end up paying more.

A T&M fee structure needs a clear and complete scope of work, as well as robust pricing assumptions from the consultant. Lacking either will complicate discussions on increases in cost and may lead to eliminating parts of the scope of work, or increasing the budget for the work. Presumably, fee structure was decided when the budget discussion took place with the CFO, and any risks with a T&M fees were raised and acceptable.

Consultants may also wish reserve the right to increase their hourly rates if the project spans more than one of their fiscal years. This may or may not be acceptable to your stakeholders, and discussion around that approach will factor into the budget and cash flow discussions you have with the CFO.

2. **Lump sum (fixed fee)**
This fee structure is "all inclusive." That is, the consultant gives a cost for a clearly defined scope of work and it is their responsibility to complete the work for the amount stated.

Lump sum costs are generally calculated based on hourly rates, the difference being that you will not see the hourly rate calculation or any line items. You will get one price for the work and unless you add scope during the project, that is what the project will cost.

Lump sums put much more risk on the consultant to manage their approach and resources within the stated cost. The kicker to this is if the consultant finds a way to do the work more efficiently than they originally thought, you don't get any money back. They keep the full amount and their profit on this work increases.

The complicated part comes if some scope is eliminated. Many consultants will argue that the price was all inclusive and it is difficult to figure out what the eliminated piece of scope costs. In a scope reduction case you have your negotiating work cut out for you.

Think of it this way: the consultant has proposed a lump sum to do the work based on agreed upon contract scope, schedule, and deliverables. The consultant is then in charge of how the work gets done. If they use more resources to complete a portion of the work than they estimated, it is not your responsibility to pay more for the project (unless you added scope).

That is the biggest risk to a consultant in a lump sum contract – their ability to manage their work in a way that makes them a profit. Lump sum fee structures are appealing for many companies because the risk sits with the consultant to do the work at the cost stated.

Lump sum should be carefully accepted and only if the scope of work is tight and the consultant has given you a good set of assumptions around their pricing. Here's a secret: most consultants don't like lump sum pricing.

If you find that your management wants you to accept a lump sum price, the Five Languages can help. Posing the decision in terms of **Finance**, you can give a summary of the assumptions and scope of work to show the relative risk to the company of a lump sum. If the scope and assumptions are loose, the risk to the company will increase. If they are tight, that is a good justification for taking a lump sum price.

3. **Milestone billing**

   Milestone billing is a project cost set to a schedule, typically based on time and materials pricing. Milestones mark the completion of different stages of the scope of work. It can be a percentage of the total cost, a specified amount when a certain deliverable is due, or a combination of both.

   The risk of this type of fee structure goes back to the risks of time and materials compounded by the possibility of delays caused by you. Most milestone billing contracts include a delay clause which requires you to pay them at the milestone billing date even though they haven't completed their work for the milestone period because you delayed them.

   Delays of this type include late information, lack of decision making, changing your mind, or failure by another company team member to do their work. The goal of the delay clause is to keep the client moving to decisions or completing their part of the work with financial penalty for dragging their feet. Hopefully, this is where the consultant will exercise their knowledge of your decision making culture and the Five Languages.

For example: in completing an upcoming milestone deliverable for a project, the consultant needs some financial information to analyze a department's performance. During the gathering of that information, the accounting department discovers they had been depreciating something incorrectly against that particular department's profit & loss statement (P&L) and they must adjust it.

The information will take longer to get, thus delaying the consultant in their assessment. Completion of the milestone deliverable, a financial model, is delayed by this correction. By contract, the consultant has the right to bill for the milestone even if the model is unfinished. It doesn't allow them to not do it – it simply lets them bill for work they haven't completed yet at the time it was originally due.

This kind of clause is not always desirable in contracts because delay is very subjective. If you must have a delay clause, be very specific about what is meant by delay. Then agree on an approach to delays neither side can control and what that means to the milestone payments.

All these terms are about the risk to the company or the consultant. The sales cycle / contract project scope, an assessment and recommendation, isn't high risk work. Fee structure may not be an issue and the decision on what fee structure to accept may rest in the timing to get the work done and how decisions are made to get there.

Changes to the Scope of Work

Changes are often a tough subject. You and the consultant will have to set expectations around how changes are communicated, approved, and noted. The possibility of change is a great opportunity to talk to the consultant about what information you and your organization need to make decisions.

Scope change conversations are an opportunity to demonstrate the languages of **Finance**, **Strategy** and **Execution**. The consultant then learns what cost, schedule and other information they need to provide, the timeframe for decision making, and how it will best be heard. Be sure you know how the pricing works, what will drive changes (in cost and schedule), and how those are addressed to the best of your ability before the work starts. Once the change conversation occurs, memorialize the results in the contract – these actions will go a long way to reducing tension over cost and change decisions in the future.

Other Contract Considerations

Non-Solicitation

Sometimes, a consultant goes to work for a client, the client really likes one of their team and wants to hire them. Conversely, a Desk employee could decide they are really interested in working for the consultant. This can create some risk to the project in either case. Since the COO at Desk is responsible for resources at the company, a conversation in the language of **Strategy** or **Execution** will be critical to deciding on using a non-solicitation clause.

There are several scenarios a consultant and client might encounter when a consultant is hired to work on a project:

1. The client recruits one of the consultant's team members.
2. The consultant recruits one of the client's team members.
3. The client's employee approaches the consultant about a job.
4. The consultant's employee approaches the client about a job.

A way to deal with the possibility of any of these situations is to include a non-solicitation clause in the contract. This clause typically outlines a time frame for recruitment, such as the length of time of the project plus six months or a year.

The clause may also specify employees or categories of employees (e.g., by title, skill, or salary level) the clause covers. Including the clause is a good way to address the issue up front and let everyone know that hiring each other's employees, no matter the circumstances, is not a desired practice.

A non-solicitation clause discussion lays the groundwork for both you and the consultant to talk to employees about what the contract says and how things might work if any of the above scenarios occur. Having a consultant compete for a position on your team can make it a little awkward for you if there isn't a vehicle for open and honest communication about the situation.

From the consultant's point of view, it might be a very strategic move for them to have a former employee in their client's office. You will need to consider all the pros and cons of hiring a consultant's employee carefully.

An approach in the situation of the client hiring one of a consultant's staff is to include a buy-out clause in the contract. A buy-out clause helps make the consultant whole for hiring the resource, although it may or may not solve any challenges to completing the work (assuming the person is going to work on something else for the client).

People need to work where they want to, and recruitment happens where it happens. It is advisable to make sure the conversation occurs and there is an agreement on how these situations will be handled before they happen.

Consider carefully the impacts of hiring a team member from your consultant while they are working on a project for you. That hire could remove critical expertise from the team that the consultant does not have elsewhere in their company. There is a great deal of risk to both your project and the consultant in this case.

There is one last proposed clause, and this is one you might not see often.

Anti-Terrorism Clause

If your company works on contracts involving Local, State or Federal funds, chances are you might need an Anti-Terrorism clause in your contract. I've seen this be an issue and while it might make your eyes pop out, it can be a consideration when hiring a consultant.

Based on the events in the U.S. on 9/11, the Patriot Act of 2001 imposes penalties for providing material support or resources to be used in terrorist acts or by foreign terrorist organizations. There is a published list of the persons and entities available through the Office of Foreign Assets Control website.

An Anti-Terrorism clause may not be required, however, a conversation with your COO or legal department will help develop the strategy around the use of one. You can control what your company does and who they work with, but you cannot control who a consultant works with. A clause requiring the consultant to comply with the Anti-Terrorism act is a good way to deal with any questions.

Advice from procurement and legal counsel is critical when developing or negotiating contracts in order to make sure subtleties of governing law or company rules are included. You must be aware of contract terms and conditions (which can be changed and how). In the case of using your consultant's contract, careful consideration must be given to how favorable terms are for Desk, and if there are clauses in the contract that protect Desk in the way they need to be protected. After all that, another discussion on an in-house contract may be needed!

Chapter 8 – Project Activities

Project Questions

What has already been done?
What needs to be done?
What decisions have been made?
What decisions will be needed?
Challenges to decision making?
Languages needed?

All the hard work of defining the problem, deciding on the approach to solving it, and finding a consultant to assist with the solution is done. A contract has been negotiated and set in place. Now it is time to get the project rolling.

At the beginning of this book, I mentioned that project management is about relationships and managing the promises made. Decisions are a form of promise and the relationships needed to help make those decisions are developed and strengthened through the Five Languages of business. All those decisions have led to the project and it is time to get into the details. Here is what comes next:

- Developing and managing project communications.
- Kicking off the project.
- Setting expectations and driving decisions on scope changes, schedule, budget, project team members (verifying the RACI).

- Deciding on project reporting and meeting timing.

Since many of the project tasks have already been discussed and double discussed, there may only be a few challenges with the RACI review. Project team members who worked on the RFP process may no longer need to be as front and center as they were, moving instead to an "Informed" or "Consulted" role. Communications may also offer some challenges, as there may be differing ideas on the Desk management team about who should put project communications out. As a PM, your skills with the Five Languages may be put to the test.

Project Kick-off Communications

Kick-off communications let the company know the project is starting, what the project is, why it is being done, the expected schedule for completion, the possible implementation option, and who the project manager and stakeholders are. The RFP has taken some time and the original problem discussion may be a faint memory for some. Things that are not right in front of people tend to be forgotten or pushed aside by demands of keeping up with day-to-day work.

The communication of the project kick-off will include high-level information in the language of **Finance**, **Strategy** and **Execution** – similar to what you presented to the CEO, CFO and COO in problem identification and justification for the consultant hire. This information will give those who need to engage in (or may be affected by) the project a deeper understanding of why the project is occurring and what changes might occur as a result.

Information provided in project kick-off communications should follow your company's approach to release financial or other data to employees. In general however, enough detail needs to be provided so those involved or affected understand the business reasons for the project. Additionally, all communications from this point forward set the stage for any change that might occur as an outcome of the project.

The key decision at this point is where the communication will come from. Most likely, the key stakeholders (the COO and CFO, as you might recollect) will need to determine which of them is best to send the communication. There are several factors to consider and discuss. The first is that the end result of the project may cause changes in the way sales does things.

While the languages of **Finance** and **Execution** may be used to come to a decision about communication of the project information, the language of **Change** will be called into use to explain the need for the change, what the benefit is to the employees, and how they will be prepared or trained to work in a different way. Even though it seems everyone agrees the sales cycle is too long and it would be much better for the company to shorten it, people directly affected by the changes the consultant comes up with may not want to buy in to those changes.

The CIO at Desk is well versed in the people side of change management and will most likely want to contribute to the communication about change. You might have been wondering about the language of **Change** – don't worry, there will be more than enough on that language!

Getting the Message Out

Since the sales contract problem is significant to Desk and the project is critical to realizing the vision of the CEO, a conversation with the COO, CIO and CFO about the different ways to publicize the project will most likely be in the languages of **Strategy**, **Execution**, and **Change**. In terms of the language of **Strategy**, this is a conversation about what tools to use, their relative value in getting the message across, and possible risks of using one or more versus others.

In the **Execution** discussion you will need to cover the *how* of getting the messages out – what resources are to be used, or if meetings need to be scheduled. Finally, in the language of **Change**, you will most likely need to educate the COO and CFO on addressing the employees about the need for the change, and what will happen with and to them because of it. In addition, the critical nature of the COO or CFO staying visible and engaged throughout the project will need to be covered here.

The amount and types of conversations above are because people take in and comprehend information differently. There are many varied approaches to getting kick-off information out to people. While there is no ultimate best practice tool to use, very typically, the preferred way is email. It is one of the simplest and reaches the most people at one time. However, people take in information much differently based on their learning style: visual, logical, aural (sound), verbal, physical, social, or solitary. These styles guide the way people recall information and the way they represent experiences.

Because this project affects sales and the sales manager, legal, the COO, the CFO, and the CEO, the decision for delivering the messaging is to have a group meeting with those people. The goal of a group meeting is to make sure the attendees see the body language of the message deliverer. Desk has no remote offices, so other resources are not needed (although a teleconference could be one of the options in that case). Additionally, the CEO decides based on the change discussions, an all-company email will be sent so people are made aware of it on peripheral levels.

An option for discussion when deciding how to message the project and the kick-off could be how to deal with those who might challenge the need for the project. This is also related to change management in that those who challenge a project may be doing so out of fear of perceived changes the project will bring, or a lack of understanding of the project. They may challenge you publicly or privately. To help resolve their worries, an approach might be to meet with them individually to find out their concerns, reiterate what you need from them, and what you can do to help them engage.

In the context of the Five Languages: What are they concerned about? What is the risk to them? What does success look like? What is in the project for them? If they are leaders of departments or divisions, talk with them about how the project outcome might support their business vision or the changes the project drives, and how you can help them and their people be ready for it.

Communications take a lot of work. For that reason, some PMs put them on the back burner. Don't fall into this trap! So many projects meet barriers and some fail due to lack of engagement of participants and stakeholders. Communication is key, and the project kick-off is the foundation of the communications for your project. Everything said is rooted in the Five Languages. It's not just for getting decisions made, it is also for communicating in a way that tells people you have heard them.

RACI Revisions

One of the key decisions for the project is the make-up and responsibilities of the project team. This team will be different from the team that handled the RFP process. One of the largest differences is the addition of the consultant to the team. It may be that the original RACI referred only to the RFP process; it will now need to be redone to focus on the project.

It is a good time to talk about decision making and ensure anyone with a C or I designation understands their involvement with decisions. The challenges to deciding on a revised RACI may come in a couple of forms: first, who is accountable or responsible and why. Second, how to deal with an important team member who cannot participate.

In the case of a team member who cannot participate, the options and consequences conversation can come in handy. In terms of the language of **Execution**, their participation can be discussed and decided on based on the risk of the lack of participation. Additionally, an examination of their overarching role in the project, stake they have in the outcome of the project, the consequences of not filling the needed role, and any alternatives to the issues can be made in this discussion. Of course, you can always tell the stakeholder that their lack of participation means the project outcomes will happen *to* them, not *for* them. (This may not be the best tactic, so use it sparingly.)

Instead, a great decision point might be centred on the use of a proxy; someone that can serve as a day-to-day representative and communicate needed decisions back and forth to the stakeholder with authority. Using the Five Languages, revisit the vision of the project, including what the problem is and what it might look like to have it solved. Remind them of the current impacts, what the benefits are when the project finishes, and what might be different in their day-to-day life when the problem no longer exists.

This can be inspiring enough to cause people to reconsider their involvement. The idea of a proxy is for a trusted right-hand person to act in the role of the stakeholder and bring their votes or decisions to the team for them. It takes some communication and time to carry this out, but this approach can free up a majority of the project time demand for the stakeholder and focus their effort where the project needs it.

Project Kick-off Meeting

The project kick-off meeting brings the project team together and sets the expectations for the project, and decision making processes. There are a lot of decisions that get made during a project – the language of **Vision** is a good tool for the basis of the project kick-off and there are some critical items to cover in the meeting.

Problem Statement and Goals

Simply put, this is a reiteration of the problem identified in Chapter 2 and the business reasons (in the language of **Vision**, **Finance** or **Execution**) for the problem needing to be solved. Because there has been a span of time between identification of the problem and the project kick-off, stakeholders and other project participants may not fully remember what set the stage for the project.

Consultant Introductions and Scope of Work Review

Since the consultant's scope of work involves an assessment, most likely they will be meeting with people to get background and information to confirm the problem. You want project participants to know who they are – have the consultant bring their key team members or the people most likely to be seen during the project.

The consultant is there to meet project participants and start to learn about your organization for their assessment. Conversely, the project participants (including stakeholders) are there to become clear about the scope of work, project timing and outcomes, and to define what success looks like. This is a great opportunity for the consultant to begin to understand the company, the culture of decision making, and listen for your use of the Five Languages of Business.

Review of the project scope is not a detailed, line-by-line examination of every iota of scope or how it will be done. Start with the high level activities and let the team ask for more information as they need it. Everyone needs a different level of detail to be comfortable with what is going to take place. You can divide the differences in to whys, whats, and hows using the languages of **Vision**, **Strategy** and **Execution**. Beginning with "why" helps to set the context of the need and the vision for the project.

This filters out a portion of the people who, once they understand why something is being done, don't need more information. Moving to the "what" (or strategy), if they know what will happen during the project, no more information about scope may be needed. The "how" people will want to know the plan – how the consultant has proposed to conduct the assessment and other project work (execution).

Keeping the discussion to a high level about why, what, and how means the project kick-off meeting can be a simple reminder of what the consultant will do, why they are doing it, and what they will produce at the end.

Schedule Review

Now that everyone is on board with the problem statement, project outcomes and scope, and the RACI has been confirmed, the project plan and schedule needs to be reviewed. The scope of work included what the consultant was going to do and deliver in the project. The project plan and schedule covers the how and when. Sometimes, the plan is the schedule. In the case of Desk's sales cycle / contract problem, assume they are one.

There are instances where stakeholders or other team members have agreed to play a role and realize they cannot do it in the needed timeframe. The discussion will then need to go back around to what might be in the way, what's changed for them since the inception of the project, and the original schedule.

Using the language of **Execution**, determine if a proxy is available or someone else with the expertise that can take the team member's place. Many things can happen between the identification of a problem and starting a project to solve it: a market shift, change in clients, emergency expenditures, or a change in strategy.

The magic of project management and the Five Languages is that they keep all those pieces moving and maintain the changes down the line. Recalling that project management is about managing the promises to be kept, the Five Languages are key to the relationships around those promises. Translating the needs of the project into the language that makes the most sense to your stakeholder or decision maker helps communicate what is needed to support the promises they made.

Progress Reporting

Another decision discussion in the kick-off meeting is the timing and content of project reporting. All projects represent some kind of financial risk both from the cost of doing the project and the cost of delays in the project. This is an opportunity for you, and the consultant, to learn the information needed for the COO and the CFO to make decisions, and what languages they think in.

Progress reports communicate status and set expectations as the project goes along. These reports show where the project is against schedule and budget. They contain information on any challenges the consultant has come up against, anything where the project might be ahead or behind, successful completion of part of the work, or any other information your company needs to stay engaged with the project. All of this information can be delivered in any of the Five Languages.

You may need to format your progress reports for several different types of readers based on the RACI. Deciding on the depth of information in the report will be a challenge, as everyone will want to see the information in different ways. The language of **Execution** may be used to make that decision – do the stakeholders want you, as the PM, to spend all your time reporting or actually getting the project done?

A portion of the report will be to inform only – a task has been completed or a decision point reached and the decision made. A portion will be to provide information for decisions – options for a change to scope and cost or schedule, for example. A portion will summarize the current status of the project and what will happen next.

Project Meetings

Some PMs enjoy meetings – I don't, particularly. One of the decisions needed from the project team is if the project needs meetings and, if so, what kind. Again, in the language of **Execution**, this is a discussion of the resource demands and how the project is going to be managed.

Stand-up meetings[12] are a fast and focused way to get pertinent information and confirm the movement of the project. A stand up is a simple, 15-minute status meeting involving all project team members with current or pending responsibilities. No one is allowed to sit down during these meetings.

Stand-ups are fast, focused sessions to review what was delivered at the end of the last week, what is going on that week, any challenges seen, what is ahead of or behind schedule, what help is needed, and what will deliver at the end of the current week. The results of the stand-up can lead to more focused meetings about specific challenges or issues with smaller groups so the entire project team doesn't need to spend their time on something that doesn't involve them.

To use a sports analogy, a stand-up meeting is a lot like a rugby scrum (with less pushing) or an American football huddle. Progress reporting puts the stand-up meeting information, schedule status, and other information into writing so stakeholders and other team members can review it at their leisure.

---

[12]Stand up meetings are used to keep meeting short (no one sits down). Today they are typically used in Agile software development processes but work with almost any meeting demand

As much as you may experience "death by meeting" at your company, some meetings should not be left out of your approach. Remember, project management is as much about making sure promises are kept as it is about making sure all tasks are on track. Giving the CEO, CFO, COO and CIO the information to make sure they can keep their promises drives the idea of having in-person progress meetings with them.

These meetings can be short and focused, much like stand-ups, and would cover the contents of the progress report, focusing on all the information they need, in their language, to understand the project budget and schedule, as well as what you might need from them.

Schedule Management

If in a stand-up meeting you are alerted to the possibility of a schedule problem or delay, the languages of **Execution**, **Finance** and **Strategy** will come into play, both when getting information from the consultant and communicating the nature and cost of the delay to the CFO. The key for you is that the consultant can articulate the nature of the anticipated delay, the plan to mitigate it, any costs to avoid the delay, and what decision is needed to implement the mitigation plan.

All the conversations they have been in as you have given examples of your company's culture of decision making have hopefully rubbed off. An ability to speak *your* Five Languages raises the value of the consultant, and makes your job more straightforward when you must take decisions up the line.

Having the consultant ahead of schedule can also impact your carefully laid out cash flow projections and trigger a conversation with the CFO. Let's say, based on the original project schedule, you set the expectation with the CFO the consultant will be paid $10,000 at the end of April. In May, the cash flow projection states the consultant will be paid $15,000 in accordance with the project plan hours and deliverables. All of a sudden the consultant is ahead; they have completed $12,000 worth of work in April.

Your company is expecting to pay $10,000. The cash "demand" has increased by $2,000. That $2,000 difference, depending on how sensitive cash flow is, may not be available. In that case, the company may have to do something with an investment they don't want to do, or it may affect another project payment. Being cognizant of what being ahead of schedule means to the company financially can help you mitigate this situation.

You cannot anticipate every situation as every project has different demands and schedules. Chapter 7 gave many insights on contract clauses and negotiations. That is the place to have conversations with the consultant to understand how they will manage schedule changes. These real life things happen. It is imperative to know and agree early to a plan B for managing real life impacts.

Budget Management

Schedule and scope changes have the most impact to the project budget. The RFP process set the budget for the sales cycle / contract problem project, and during approval conversations with the CFO you were able to include some contingency in the budget. Spending contingency needs to be mutually agreed between you and the CFO. Adequately communicating the costs of changes will take the language of **Finance**, and possibly **Strategy**.

For example's sake, assume that the consultant's contract ended up as a milestone billing based on a lump sum for the work, with a delay clause on the billing. Lump sum contracts place the risk on the consultant to manage their staff within the contract amount for the project, or risk losing profit. You had the conversation with the consultant during contract negotiations about how they would manage schedule changes based on their internal issues, and you know what will happen if your company delays the consultant's work.

Budget Changes

The project team will need to decide how budget changes will be handled. Additional needed scope is probably the easiest to deal with. It could be that as the consultant is working, they discover another group is impacted by the problem and they need to extend their assessment interviews to include that group. It is time to go back to the conditions of the consultant contract – while their contract is a lump sum, assume you negotiated that all changes to the contract would be at hourly rates.

The change will be simple for the consultant to articulate. It will consist of the hours, billing rate, and total estimated cost for adding interviews. When taking it to the CFO for approval, you will need to articulate the need for the change in percentage of total project cost, why the change is needed in business terms (rather than in terms of the consultant's work), any anticipated benefits of adding the work, as well as the risks of not adding the work.

Scope creep (uncontrolled changes or continuous growth in the scope) is the most difficult to manage and communicate. Uncontrolled changes can come from almost anywhere, the most common being the stakeholders or other project team members. Unfortunately, these are usually ones you hear about last.

Call to mind that the consultant is interviewing people across the company as part of their assessment of the sales cycle problem. Perhaps, as they talk with legal during the project, they are asked to perform some research on a specific topic discussed. And they do it. The research is not part of the baseline scope, nor something you have agreed to with them.

Going back to contract negotiations – conversations about the process of validating requests for additional work should have been included. In the language of **Execution**, the consultant needs to be reminded of the process for changes, authority levels for changes, and what information is needed to make decisions around the changes.

In this case, assume the need for the research is validated. You can then go back to the needed scope conversation with the CFO. If the request for research turns out to be based in convenience, the conversation may then turn to using the requestor's existing budget to pay for the work. Worst case, as a way of making a point, you may not pay the consultant for the work done. I hate when that has to happen.

The kick-off meeting helps confirm that the problem was still the problem, the scope of work will get you to the outcome you want, and the consultant knows what success looks like. The consultant is going to perform the scope of work of the project. As the PM, you will manage communications and decision conversations, the schedule, and any scope changes.

The list seems simple, I assure you it is not. Recall that project management is not only making sure everyone is doing what they need to do, when they need to do it, it is also about making sure promises are kept. The Five Languages are one of the toolsets tailor made to help you do this.

Chapter 9 – Project Results

Project Questions

What has already been done?

What needs to be done?

What decisions have been made?

What decisions will be needed?

Challenges to decision making?

Languages needed?

Now we are getting down to the end. As a result of many conversations in the Five Languages, decisions have been made and built upon. The problem was identified: our fictional company, Desk, has a sales contracting cycle that is impacting recognition of revenue. The effect is the company is not able to grow in the way Desk's CEO envisions.

A project was initiated to solve the problem, resulting in selection of an internal PM and an external consultant. The consultant's work was to confirm the problem is really the problem, assess the problem, and develop a solution to solve it.

Earlier discussions with the CFO and COO led to the decision to set the budget for the project through the RFP process, as well as leave the implementation pricing until the assessment was done. The goal of leaving implementation pricing and work for later is to determine if the budget is available to have the consultant do that work, or if the work would be done in-house. The project kick-off and all the coordination, expectations, and decisions coming from that meeting were memorialized.

Skipping ahead from the kick-off meeting, you, the project team, and the consultant have worked hard at the assessment of the sales cycle / contract problem. The consultant validated the problem and its impacts were in alignment with the original problem statement. The assessment has revealed good information, and the consultant has drafted a recommendation to solve the problem (along with a proposed project to implement the solution).

Now, the project team will need to engage in discussions about what information to present, how to present the information, and to whom. Along with those decisions come others, such as when information is sent out, who will present, and what to do if there are challenges to the recommendation.

First though, let's go through how the consultant might have gotten to their recommendation. Remember, *how* they do their work has been left to them, *what* was wanted from their work was defined by Desk's RFP and project teams.

Gap Analysis

One of the ways to get to a solution is to engage in a gap analysis[13]. Recall that the recommendation resulting from this project defines the implementation of actions/initiatives to solve the sales contract problem. Simply put, a gap analysis defines where you are, where you want to be and how you will get there.

The assessment of the sales cycle problem gives the current state: a long sales cycle that leads to delayed revenue recognition, delayed commissions, and uses a lot of salespeople's time that could be better spent garnering more sales. Additionally, the assessment has revealed that part, if not all, of the long cycle is due to contract negotiations as defined originally. It appears the contract salespeople are using is dated, and because of outdated terms a majority of clients want the contract changed every time it is used.

The future need, simply stated, is a shorter sales cycle supported by a simple-to-negotiate contract. Based on the assessment results, there may be a certain cycle length or type of contract desired in the

---

[13] See **http://robdkelly.com/blog/getting-things-done/gap-analysis/** for a simple explanation of gap analysis.

future, and training, contract revision, or other activities needed to get there. The recommendation will take the results of the gap analysis and develop the project activities to get from the long cycle of today to the vision of the cycle in the future.

As another example, perhaps you are dealing with a financial reporting problem identified through looking at overspending on capital projects. The problem is specific to internal capital project outlay. The visibility the CEO has of approved projects against overall budget, as well as spend to budget, on each approved project is close to zero.

Therefore, the CEO is approving projects in a vacuum, which rightfully so, makes for some nerves. The current state, as revealed by an assessment, is:

- No reporting of requested projects versus budgeted projects.
- No reporting of approved project budget versus spend.
- No one person specifically named as "owner" of reporting and cost management.
- The financial system doesn't easily and simply provide cost reporting.
- Process for project costing and approvals is not defined.
- Those accountable for the spend justification rarely fully participate in the approval process

(the approval process is slightly random and informal).

The future state could be defined as follows:

- Annual budget / spend as well as project budget / spend reporting in place.
- One person responsible for reporting and cost management for internal capital projects.
- Clearly defined and documented process for project costing and approval.
- Reporting that translates financial system data into information that supports the information need.
- Those requesting internal capital projects clearly understand their accountability to the project and their role in the approval process, and engage in both.

The third step in a gap analysis is to look at the gaps between current and future state, and outline the activities or steps it would take to get to the future state, as well as the decisions needed to get there. For the example, they could be:

- Investigate the data available from the financial system and develop a reporting template that can be populated with that data simply and easily.

- Name the accounting manager responsible for cost management and reporting.
- Develop an approval process for internal project approvals.
- Create training to educate any potential project requestor on how the process works and what is expected of them.
- Provide an opportunity for the appropriate parties to sit in the annual budgeting process for feedback on reporting and processes that support use of the budget.

The activities getting you from current to future state are changes from status quo. The changes they create will necessitate using the language of **Change** when reviewing the recommendation. For instance, project requestors will need to buy in to a more formal project request process. You will need to help them understand the reason for the process change and what is in it for them. Then, you will have to use the language of **Change** to coach executive management in supporting, evangelizing, and reinforcing (rewarding) the continued participation in the new process.

You can see how a gap analysis supports the recommendation of a solution by linking current state to future state. The items identified to get from current to future also start to define the conversations around the activities in terms of the Five Languages.

How Many Recommendation Reviews?

Ideally, one review of the recommendation would be all that is needed. However, giving key stakeholders and decision makers a first pass through any significant project result can increase the likelihood of the result being accepted.

In this case, you are looking for approval of the consultant's recommendation. Depending on the protocols in your company, you may need to take the assessment and recommendation through the CEO, CFO, COO or CIO before presenting it to the rest of the company.

A key decision is how many times you will ask for feedback on the recommendation before presenting the solution for final approval. Remember, there is some urgency to solving this problem and the key stakeholder group is fairly small. In some companies, the key stakeholders may range all over the company, so more review may be needed.

In Desk's case, working with the COO and CFO on the number of reviews in the language of **Execution** and **Finance** is probably the ticket. Weighing the benefits of the resources (time and people) needed against the desire to get the problem solved is one consideration. Making sure everyone is on board with the solution and the changes needed to implement it may outweigh the need for a speedy resolution, depending on how complicated the solution is.

There are three possible information reviews: draft, draft final, and final. This might seem a little like overkill – it depends on the culture of decision making at your company. Without passing judgement on any culture, the larger or more consensus-driven the company is, the more reviews are likely to be needed just because of the sheer number of people that need to decide or weigh in.

Because the stakeholders and decision makers know the organization well, having them give feedback on the thinking behind the recommendation can help identify any unintended consequences of the solution. Additionally, feedback can help you make sure any recent or upcoming strategies are not impacted.

Feedback makes every product better – a stakeholder might build on the consultant's observations or give insight to changes elsewhere in the company to improve the recommended solution. This is a great opportunity for both you and the consultant to learn more about what language company constituents think in.

There are some possible challenges to the decision to release the recommendation to the greater company. Let's say the draft recommendation is sent out and response from critical stakeholders is low. There could be a couple possible scenarios of why that has occurred.

The first reason may be because of the quality of communications throughout the project, they understand and agree with the problem statement, the business impacts of the problem, the benefit/cost of doing the project to solve it, and how the solution might support their vision for their department/division or the company. They trust that the recommendation is sound because you have kept them up to speed in a language they speak.

The second reason may be that they are too busy or not interested enough to respond. For those that are too busy, the conversation will be based in the language of **Vision** and the impacts of the lack of feedback. The theme will be how not responding may affect achievement of their vision for the company or their department/division.

Simply put, if they don't respond there will be no place to complain when the outcome of implementing the recommendation happens *to* them. Disinterest could mean they understand the recommendation and don't have need or interest in responding with feedback. I have found the conversation in the language of **Vision** will get attention both from those that are too busy and those who say they aren't interested.

In all of this, the communication of the recommendation is critical. Throughout the project work, opportunities have arisen for the consultant to learn how to bring information forward and in what language. The information surrounding the recommendation has, with a bit of foresight and a lot of editing, been spoken to the stakeholders in the way they think, in a way they can hear and accept the recommendation.

Think about it this way: the recommendation is a vision you are putting forward. A recommendation can certainly be put in front of stakeholders without first sending a draft for review and feedback. That approach has the potential to surprise people because the consultant might be making an innovative or hard-hitting recommendation with perceived negative impacts.

It could be that during the time of the assessment another department or division launched an initiative that is completely opposed to what the consultant recommends because of changing circumstances or something they just didn't know.

On the positive side, giving a draft recommendation may validate something another department or division was trying to do in parallel. It gives someone else validation from an outside source that they were thinking along the right lines. You may also be able to discern some of the other party's thinking to see if they had ideas which might improve your solution.

Draft Final Recommendations

The draft recommendation is a chance to test the outcome of the sales cycle assessment with stakeholders and decision makers. That step allows you to gather feedback on the draft, assure the current and future state are correct, and validate any assumptions made in developing the solution. You may also have gained insight on any other changes in company strategy or approach that might impact the proposed solution.

Preparing the draft final recommendation and sending it back to the group that provided feedback is a way to assure them their comments were heard and included. If their comments were not included, the draft final recommendation is a way to tell them why. Experience shows it is better to make sure people know they have been heard than to let them assume they have not.

The Five Languages can be used to help stakeholders understand why their comments were not included. Choosing from **Vision**, **Finance**, **Execution**, **Change**, or **Strategy** gives you a way to articulate the reasons in terms of business. Excluding a comment or suggestion doesn't mean it is bad, the comment or suggestion needs to meet the business need around strategic vision, financial health, operational excellence, or buy-in to change.

Everyone has had their say, any adjustments that have to happen at that final draft stage were made. Now it is time to present the recommendation and get a decision made on the implementation.

Presentation Decisions

There are decisions on the recommendation presentation that are more tactical than anything, and probably don't require the Five Languages to make. For reference they are: where, when, who comes, how long is needed, and who will make the final decision on the recommendation if the meeting comes to an impasse.

Depending again on the culture of decision making at the company, who comes and who makes the final decision may be a matter of a discussion in the language of **Strategy**. One other key decision is who presents the information to the decision making group.

Presenters

Who presents the recommendation in the meeting is not always a question. Usually the PM is the presenter, especially since they may know and speak the Five Languages of the key stakeholders and decision makers better than anyone else. However, not everyone is great at presenting.

A second choice might be to have the consultant present, particularly if presentation is not your strong suit. There is risk with choosing the consultant to present: they may not have as firm a grasp on which of the Five Languages are needed for the presentation.

Equally, there are certain benefits to having the consultant present, as they know the recommendation intimately – after all, they developed it. This approach can be described as presenting in partnership with the role of consultant as the expert on the recommendation and the role of the PM as the business expert, providing details in the Five Languages of business drivers, cost, timing, or thinking behind the recommendation.

You can also consider having a stakeholder do the presentation. This is a slightly risky approach as they may not be as well versed in the details (unless they've been closely aligned with the project all along). There is also some danger that they will present at too high a level or they will try to influence the recommendation in some way.

Additionally, if the stakeholder doesn't know the recommendation or project as intimately as the consultant or you, the presentation might not be as well received as needed. Also, they may not understand the subtleties of the Five Languages as well as you and the consultant, creating the risk of all your hard work in communications being minimized.

The Presentation

A very important reminder: the Five Languages are about business and are based in the different ways company leaders think and talk about the business. Business is not personal and the Five Languages help keep the perspective on the business rather than on the person. Think about what Desk is trying to do. The sales manager has noticed the issues that come from a long sales cycle are affecting the business and his statement of the original problem was in the context of effect.

He was lucky enough to understand all Five Languages and communicate in them well enough to get the problem solved. As you move into the final presentation of the recommendation, keep the previous thought in mind – it will help if you run into problems getting the decision made.

Starting the meetings with context for the attendees is an excellent way to set the business tone (the purpose, objectives, givens, and scope of the meeting)[14]. The purpose is simple – why everyone is in the room. This can be delivered in the languages of **Strategy** and **Vision**. In the case of the Desk sales cycle project, it is to review the consultant's recommendation and make a decision on implementing the solution they have devised so the vision of the CEO can be realized.

Objectives are what is to be accomplished in the meeting, also delivered in the language of **Strategy**. These include what the issue was and what the expected results were. Givens of the meeting are what you expect of the participants. For example, computers and phones off, full engagement, etc. These

---

[14] Also known as POGS (Purpose, Objectives, Givens, Scope)

can be delivered in the language of **Vision**: your vision for how people participate.

Scope of the meeting outlines the boundary of what will be discussed in the meeting. By way of example, discussion of the strategy for the next year's manufacturing equipment is probably not within the scope of a meeting to decide on implementing a project to solve the sales cycle issue. I've seen odder things come up that threw everything off track!

The presentation includes the options for implementation, as well as the consequences of those options for the attendees to consider. Since you have had meetings about the recommendations and heard comments on the presentation through the draft process you most likely know, in terms of the Five Languages, what questions will be asked.

Taking the time in advance to anticipate questions, based on what you know about attendees and the information they need, will help capture a good percentage of the questions arising. Anticipating questions is an intuitive exercise that gets simpler as you become more practiced at the Five Languages your company speaks.

If you cannot come up with questions you think will be asked, talk to those on the project who work for the key stakeholders and decision makers. Project team members may have the best insight into what information their management needs. You will probably succeed in getting about 80 percent of the questions that might be asked. It is a great time to consider which of the Five Languages you will need to use.

Challenges in the Presentation

Here is where the basis of the Five Languages in business really starts to pay off. A big challenge in presentations that I have encountered, especially when a decision is needed on a lot of detailed information, is rat-holing[15]. The presentation gets dragged off track by someone that wants to pursue a particular angle or detail possibly unrelated to the subject at hand. The group then ends up talking about something unrelated to the recommendation and decision you are trying to get made.

The information covered in the meeting opening, especially the scope of the meeting, is a tool to help keep meetings on track and prevent (or give a way to prevent) any rat-holing that might occur.

The meeting scope review informs attendees of

---

[15] Urban Dictionary definition: to digress in an extensive way or when a conversation follows a constant tangent and ends up with a topic that has nothing to do with the original discussion.

what will, and will not, be discussed in the meeting. If there is someone pulling the conversation off track you can go back to the scope of the meeting and remind them of the meeting boundaries. An offer of having the sideline discussion after the meeting is a reasonable compromise.

Another challenge is the bomb question: one that is designed to disrupt the decision process. If the question truly stops the decision in its tracks, you may want to turn to the key stakeholders and decision makers for a response on how they want to continue.

If possible, pose it in options and consequences, bringing back in the appropriate language with the accurate information for the consequences. Depending on the answer, the meeting may continue and you come to resolution and decision, or you may need to pivot and decide what happens next.

Another awkward situation can come when a question is asked and the answer isn't one the asker wants to hear. It is entirely likely that the questioner has asked the question previously, gotten an answer they don't want, and wants to air it again in public.

As someone versed in the Five Languages, you can diffuse the situation with the business reasons for the answer. Sometimes it might be that having the consultant give the answer is actually less difficult for the question-poser. People take harder answers from consultants than they do employees.

Your presentation has gone swimmingly and everyone is in agreement about the implementation of the solution to Desk's problem. Now you are about to launch the final step!

Chapter 10 - Implementation

Project Questions

What has already been done?
What needs to be done?
What decisions have been made?
What decisions will be needed?
Challenges to decision making?
Languages needed?

Much has taken place over the past chapters: many conversations and dozens of decisions, small and large. Because your pre-work was so good and you have used the Five Languages skillfully before and during the presentation, Desk's CEO, CFO, COO, CIO and sales manager have decided to go with the consultant's recommendation on how to solve the problem. Through the honing and use of the Five Languages in those processes you have gotten to the final decision – implementing the consultant's recommended solution.

The decision to implement the recommendation will start the project cycle over again, creating more decisions and choices. Similar to some previous decisions, the project team will need to choose to implement either externally or internally.

The key decision makers on the implementation team may be different from those on the assessment project. The project team will almost certainly change. And the best news is, all of these changes and decisions will require the use of the Five Languages, which you now know well!

Let's assume, because of the great communication by you and the excellent work by the consultant, the company has agreed to the following to solve the problem:

- Streamline the actual sales cycle through process rework.
- Add technology tools to automate some of the process that is currently done by hand.
- Rewrite the client contract based on feedback from negotiations and establish different levels of contracts based on the type of sale made.
- Establish a position or role to oversee sales contract negotiation, with the authority to make changes as needed to keep the negotiation moving.
- Develop and measure sales cycle key performance indicators (KPIs) to track the effectiveness of the changes.

The project will involve members of several Desk departments: sales, legal, IT and finance. Because sales sits under the COO, she will most likely be the key stakeholder. In addition, the decision has been made to continue with the current consultant and a change to their contract has been negotiated.

This negotiation came through a conversation you had with the CFO, which included: changes in ROI of project cost versus gains from a shortened sales cycle, the health of the assessment project budget, cash flow projections for the new project, and reevaluation of the risks of leaving the sales cycle the way it is. A visit to the CEO confirmed that his vision for the future of the company relies heavily on having the sales cycle problem fixed, he is in favor of the strategy, and supports the change to the consultant's contract.

The agreed upon project scope will bring one of the Five Languages into the mix that has been minimally present so far – the language of **Change**. You didn't think I forgot about it, did you? Every item of scope noted will create change of some magnitude. The sales folks will experience most of it, but legal and IT will also be affected.

This means the CIO will be an active member of the project team; at Desk he is the change management leader. The greatest challenge to the upcoming decisions will be the people affected by the changes. So, let's talk a little about change.

Change

The context of change management for the purposes of this book is focused on change as it impacts people at an individual level. Change management, especially when the result depends on people adopting the change, can be one of the most overlooked components of a project. The concept of corporate transformation challenges and change management is not new – it has been studied and written about for at least 40 years[16].

Change management practices help organizations prepare for, deal with, and continue to perform at a high level before, during, and after changes in the company. These practices also help with project adoption, which is huge if the ROI of a project depends on people adopting the results of your project. In the case of Desk's project, the need for people to adopt the new process and any automation that comes with it is relatively high. Therefore, change management activities will be important.

Dealing with the people side of change is both subtle and complicated, as you may have experienced. Many organizations rely on the "edict" method of change – an order from management should be enough for people to adopt to the change. I think you can guess how successful that method is. Another aspect to this is that project managers, by virtue of their work, are not change managers. They

---

[16] See **https://en.wikipedia.org/wiki/Change_management** for some basic information on change management

may cause change through the implementation of projects, yet their focus is on executive decisions.

Change management is about executive actions. As such, change management is a combination of securing executive sponsorship for the change, coaching the executives on communicating the need for change and the desired outcome, and helping executives stay visible and engaged throughout the realization of the change. These activities only scratch the surface. Because change management can be complicated, the biggest recommendation I can make is to call on someone from your company's change management office or find a great consultant to assist in those critical activities.

As mentioned previously, change will come about in each of the scope areas. First, the sales process rework will cause the sales folks to change how and when they do what they do. Although there may be agreement that the change is needed and good, humans really don't like when change happens…go figure. At the end of the day, the change will still be happening to the sales folks. The process changes may also affect legal as they will be asked to engage in the process differently than they do today.

Second, adding technology to automate parts of the process may test some of the sales folks' ability or desire to use the technology. Adding technology will most likely also affect IT since they will be involved with selection, installation, training on, and management of, a new tool. Modification of the current contract will require legal and sales to learn a new contract format and what can and cannot be changed.

A new role overseeing the negotiating process adds more people into the negotiation mix, altering responsibilities. Creating KPIs and putting them in place is a major change from how sales and legal have worked until now. Success measurement in legal is a new concept. Since Desk's sales reps work on commission, KPIs may be harder to apply. In other companies this may not apply and KPIs would be a great tool for success management.

The project is going to drive change from many points. For you as the PM, the language of **Change** will enable you to speak to change by providing your executives with information on the need for the changes, and how ready sales and legal are to make them. The language of **Change** will help you coach the executives or department leaders on how to bring employees along in supporting the change, any education available to increase their ability to understand or use new tools, and the things that will be done to strengthen and sustain participation in the changes.

Change Planning

In Chapter 9 there was a discussion on gap analysis and how it can help identify what needs to be *done* to get from a current state to a future state. This methodology can also be used to determine what needs to *change* to get from a current state to a future state. What works best is for both of those things to be determined and implemented at the same time.

As you know, the decision has been made to change the sales contract. The current state is that the contract is outdated and takes a long time to negotiate. The future state is to have a baseline contract and possible modifications given the type of sale being made. If you go back to Chapter 7 on contracting, some of the questions and decisions made there for the consultant's contract may be exactly the things to be discussed on the internal sales contract.

The project activities for changing the contract may be coordinating with legal for their suggestions on a new base contract and modifications, then having a set of reviews and edits, resulting in the final version of the contract. The change activities that come with this piece of scope will be very different.

In the language of **Change**, the current state for contracting in sales is "this is way we've always done it" and the future state will be a new set of contracts with new language and new negotiation approaches. Everyone outside of sales and legal may agree this will be part of speeding up negotiations, which in turn will speed up revenue recognition (a simple cause/effect example).

Inside of sales and legal, what may not be seen is the anxiety the teams have about the change to new language, having to know more about contracts, how to choose the right one, what the penalty is for not choosing the right one, and so on (and so on, and so on). When left to their own accord (read: not told directly enough what is really going on), humans will pick the worst case every, single, time.

The language of **Change** will assist you with coaching the executives involved in the process change so they can articulate the need for the change to the contracts. Having the CEO give the message that it is a move to allow the company to grow and be more robust is imperative. The sales manager and the head of legal will need guidance for their one-to-one conversations with employees to help them understand and embrace the new contracts.

The language of **Change** gives a basis to talk about the following:

- **Why the change is needed:** speed up the contract process, enable more sales, or help the company be more robust financially.

- **Gain the employees' buy in and support of the change:** when the contract process is not so slow, you can complete more sales, resulting in more commission for you while the company's financial health improves.

- **What they need to know to make the change:** contract training and education so that they don't have to worry about picking the right or wrong contract document, and how to negotiate the new contracts.

- **Giving them the opportunity to apply their learning to the new process:** the decision to have a contract point person shows that Desk is willing to put resources in the right place so everyone is successful.

- **Celebrating the success of the change:** outlining the rewards and reinforcement of employees' willingness make and sustain the change. This conversation can be held with the executives alone so they can decide how they want to positively reinforce success. A simple handwritten "thank you" may suffice in some cases. In other cases, a party, bonus, or other more visible means is appropriate.

Using these thoughts as a basis for talking about the project scope, let's take a look at some of what has been agreed upon to be done.

KPIs and Metrics

Based on the consultant's recommendation, Desk has decided to establish key performance indicators (KPIs) to monitor the success of the changes to the sales contracting process. According to Wikipedia, KPIs measure aspects of performance that are most critical for current and future success of a project and organization[17].

The characteristics of good KPIs are simplicity, comparability, and *incremental* improvement...and they need to be understandable. In other words, they should be well written with one clear measure. They should also be realistic, time framed, and define how data will be tracked. KPIs need to balance and measure inputs, the quantity and quality of work required to produce a certain output, measure the quantity or quality of the results achieved, as well as the benefit realized from the outputs (the value).

A KPI needs to be designed to deliver a message that will instigate a decision: either do nothing or

---

[17] See also David Parmenter's 7 Characteristics of Effective KPIs, http://davidparmenter.com/

check into what is going on. They tell you if things are looking bad, things are looking good, or things are ok. In the first case, an investigation and fix is needed. In the second, check out the situation and learn from what is going right. These lessons can be implemented in other areas and can keep your items that are going good from becoming outdated items that are just "ok." In the third, do nothing – everything is going ok (and that is ok).

Keep in mind that KPIs in Desk's case will be used to see if the contract and process changes are resulting in a shorter sales cycle. When developing the KPIs, decisions are needed on who the audience is, and how many will be used. A word of caution: there is usually a desire to create many KPIs because everyone wants to measure in a different way. A rule of thumb is two or three - when you hear people talking about "the most important KPIs" you have too many.

Let's go back to Desk's sales cycle problem. While discussing KPIs, the project team discovers that the shortest time frame for completing a contract is six weeks, with many taking eight or ten. A great question to help determine the KPI is, in the language of **Strategy**, "What does right look like?" Desk has an inclusive culture, so the sales folks are in on this discussion – there is nothing better than people buying into what they think success looks like.

The sales manager and his team believe that most sales contracts should take four weeks or less, based on the potential new contract documents and establishing of a new position to support contract negotiation. In this case, the KPI might look something like: Within three months of process change implementation and new document availability and training, contract completion time will average four weeks.

The decision to use a directional KPI, that is, one that measures a trend, created some animated discussion at Desk. Guiding the final decision was the language of **Execution**; the belief is there will not be an immediate improvement because people need to get used to the new documents and process. Success was defined as the sales cycle getting shorter and shorter. If this doesn't happen, or the trend slows, that is the KPI saying, "Check this out, something needs to be fixed." When that happens, another decision can be made about whether or not to check the trend and adjust the process or tool.

KPIs are a change to the way things have been done at Desk in the past. Recall that part of the reason the problem became so acute is that there was only informal tracking of the length of the sales cycle. The language of **Change** is used here because KPIs are a reinforcement tool. Executives will need to explain to people how the KPI will help Desk know if the process changes are working, and pave the way for celebration as the trend heads toward their definition of success. Tying this success back to how it impacts the success of the company (and thus, everyone) helps reinforce the benefit of the measurement.

The New Position

Another action recommended by the consultant was for Desk to establish a new position to oversee contract negotiation. The recommendation specifically called out the need for this position to have the authority to make changes to contracts when called for. Chapter 7 introduced the idea of a PM, or other party, well educated in the contract clauses that Desk is willing to allow changes in, and those that cannot change. The idea is similar for this position.

However, this position is new. In the past, the sales folks knew the contract well and negotiated their own contracts. The age of the contracts and outdated terms meant legal was often taxed by sales' needs for changes to the contract. You would think sales and legal would be glad to have someone that would negotiate contracts for them, right? Guess again.

Humans are a funny bunch (so be ready for the language of **Change** again). Think back to the beginning of this chapter where you were coaching executives on getting people to understand and buy into a change. While on an intellectual level, sales and legal may see the need for someone to handle sales contracts, in their heads they are making up a lot of bad stories. Something such as: "What if they do the job better than I do?" or "What if they make more money than I do?" and anything else someone can think of.

The language of **Change** will help you prepare the COO to have the conversations about why the change is needed, why now, the business reasons for making the change, and the benefit to the people involved in the change. Perhaps it is something like this: if the salespeople aren't the only ones negotiating contracts, they can sell more.

If they sell more, they make more in commissions. It's all about what is in it for them. For legal, it is an opportunity to reduce workload (or at least balance it). This is something they have been talking about for quite a while. The COO can even put the change in the language of **Vision** – her vision for eventually establishing a procurement group to support the entire company. Perhaps this is the first step of that vision. If she's been talking about this for a while, people will start to connect that vision with the changes that are being made.

Whatever else the change management activities are with a project, the most critical thing is for executive sponsors of the project to stay up front and visible for the duration of the project. They need to communicate repeatedly about goals of the project and why the changes are needed. And these communications need to be done in terms of the business as well as the employees.[18]

Let's leave change management for a moment and consider some of the last decisions to be made about the implementation project.

Resourcing the Project

The implementation project is a little different than the assessment project, but many of the tasks are the same. As the project plan is being developed, the internal resources needed are starting to solidify, and you will be repeating some the set up steps covered in the preceding chapters.

In the languages of **Execution** and **Strategy**, the conversation will be with the COO and CIO about how much time the project will need from their resources, who you believe is the right resource, and

---

[18] If you're interested, Prosci (www.prosci.com) has a ton of research on what is working and not working in change management.

the benefit of the resource playing a part in the outcome of the project. There will most likely also be a conversation about budget and risk. The risk conversation can utilize options and consequences to determine acceptability of any risks.

Before Action Review

Just as in the earlier effort to hire a consultant, your project team needs to understand the plans and expectations associated with the new project. A Before Action Review (BAR) is a handy way to review the plans and expectations. The BAR comes from the military, and is a process that helps a team state their intention (task, purpose, end state) while adding discipline to challenge and risks, and drawing on lessons learned from past experiences. It can also include roles and responsibilities of the players and define what success looks like.

The BAR doesn't have to be stuffy – you can address all these items in very fun ways. Bottom line, it helps everyone understand what is going on, how to get from current state to future state, and agree on what defines success. In the languages of **Strategy** and **Vision**, the BAR helps everyone understand why you are there working on this project and how it supports the strategic vision of the department, division, or company.

End result: the BAR outlines everything there is about the project and can include people you may need assistance from later in the project. It normalizes across everyone involved and synchronizes everyone with the project.

Progress Reporting

The new project for the solution is significantly more detailed and impacts groups differently than the assessment. The outcomes of process rework, technology tool implementation, a new position, and KPI establishment will drive a lot of change – and with it the need for change communication. The languages of **Finance** and **Execution**, along with **Change**, will start to come back into play in progress reporting.

Progress reporting will be geared at three or four different groups with different needs for information. In the first group, the CIO and COO will more than likely look for high-level information with an emphasis on quick review to identify areas where decisions or input are needed. For them, any risk of delay, cost increases, or change management issues will be forefront.

In this case, a stoplight format might support the need for summarized information. A stoplight format shows key areas of the project such as cost, change management issues, and schedule, and whether they are going well, have challenges, or have stopped due to a major problem. These statuses are indicated by green, yellow or red – thus the "stoplight" name.

The second group to receive progress information may be those who are secondary decision makers: the leaders of groups that report to the CIO and COO. An example of this would be the legal manager or sales manager. As the stoplight report gives summary information, they might need a little more detail so they can make decisions on resourcing or other project demands.

Key to progress reporting is agreeing on the cadence of the reporting. An easy way to set reporting cadence is to ask (before the project starts) what information is needed, how much, how often, and for whom. The answers to these questions allow you to structure reporting in a way that gives the most information to the right people in the way they want to receive it.

In order to avoid constant customization of the reporting, report to the rule (not the exception) and deal with specific information requests on a case-by-case basis. A report will collapse under its own weight and become an administrative nightmare otherwise. Keeping the information a right fit for everyone receiving the reports is a good practice of options and consequences. It also speaks to the resourcing needs or budget constraints (if any) that might preclude elaborate reporting.

All reporting decisions will certainly be discussed in the language of **Execution** – what is the right balance of resource usage versus the information needed? The key is to make sure the review is regular, the data flows into the reporting at the right level of detail, and review is timed and stated in a way that enables quick decisions for mitigating any project issues.

Calling an Audible

During every project there is a chance of encountering a challenge that takes the project off track. Many times, challenges come in the form of a change in political landscape within the company or a change in a key stakeholder. Consider a project that is running smoothly until…the leader of a department heavily impacted by the outcome of your project takes a promotion and moves to another division in the company. This happens more often than you might think.

Then a new department head is selected – they may not know the department's operations well or even be aware of the project. To bring them up to speed, you will need to gather all the information that led up to the project: problem statement, project and other plan, recommendations, and all other information that supports the project.

You may also want to bring in the other key stakeholders in the project (if any) to bring the new player up to speed on what decisions led to the project, the basis of the decisions, and the desired outcome of the project. This is a time when your skills in the Five Languages will come in handy, so you can quickly learn the new person's language.

Consider this: what happens if after all the review, the new department head decides not to continue with the project? They may need time to make sure they understand the department, or might have ideas of their own about solving the problem. At this point, you may want to see if the key decision makers through the entire process need to be gathered to help determine if you should stop the project or stay the course.

As someone well versed in the Five Languages, you can develop the options and consequences, focusing on the business impacts or benefits of each consequence as well as the language to deliver it in. In Desk's case, this discussion might be about the vision of the CEO and how the sales cycle problem affects revenue recognition.

Once the final decision is made, whether the project is stopped or the project continues with altered scope or outcomes, a summary of the discussion and record of the decision should be prepared and communicated. Communication of the continuation will be key to maintaining new agreements on scope, schedule, and outcome. All the languages will come to bear, depending on who is making the decision on the project.

Project, communication, and change management plans will also need to be altered to match the new conditions of the project. The project team will need to understand what the new lay of the land is, in terms of **Vision**, **Strategy**, **Finance** or **Execution**. The language of **Change** will come into play if the project comes to a stop and the originally anticipated changes are suspended.

If it is agreed the project needs to come to a complete stop, communication around that decision will also need to be made. You would then start back into the cycle of decision making about the problem, assessing the issues, and offering options and consequences. Business change happens – and it isn't always fun to deal with. However, when armed with the Five Languages you can deliver business justifications in the way people can hear them best.

Finishing the Project

Luckily, no key stakeholder changes have happened during Desk's sales cycle project. Approaching the end of the project takes some focus since project processes do not stop until the outcome is reached. Having a clear definition of what "finished" looks like is always helpful as project team members can start to lose focus due to heavy demands from the start of a new project or going back to their regular job. The end may get a little more intense as details are verified, deliverables reviewed, KPIs are set up, and documentation is completed.

PlusDelta Meetings

An effective way to wrap up a project and capture information even when people are losing focus is a meeting that goes by many names: PlusDelta, After Action Review, Lessons Learned, or Post Mortem. Post Mortem sounds a little morbid. I think using PlusDelta or After Action Review gives the meeting a more positive spin.

A PlusDelta or After Action Review meeting is a retrospective of you accomplished, what was supposed to happen versus what actually happened, why the differences, what worked, what didn't, and what the team might do differently in the future (thus the "delta" in PlusDelta). The languages of **Vision**, **Strategy**, and **Execution** come into play in a PlusDelta meeting. These languages help ensure the retrospective of the project ties to the original decision to do the project in the first place.

The PlusDelta at the end of project meeting focuses more on the positive (more than a Lessons Learned format). It is also a forum to go back to the definition of success and confirm the project was successful.

Customer Satisfaction Surveys

Another set of information to gather at the end of the project is how satisfied the "customers" were with the process and the project outcome. In this case, the customers are not Desk's customers, but the individuals inside the organization that were impacted by the project.

Recall the problem the sales cycle project needed to solve and who was involved with it: legal, sales, finance, IT, the COO and the CIO, among others. Getting their feedback on how the project went, how satisfied they are that the project met success criteria, and if the results were acceptable is a good measure of satisfaction. Additionally, that feedback can include how well change was handled and their sense of the effectiveness of the adoption of the changes.

All of the Five Languages may come into play in finding out how customers feel about the project. Did the project support their vision? Was it financially successful? Was communication on the project what they needed it to be? How was change handled? Was the project managed well?

In order for Desk to know if the changes made to the contract and contracting process actually work, the developed KPIs will need to be monitored as well. In terms of the language of **Execution**, choosing who will monitor this will come down to resources available. The COO will most likely want to own that since sales works for her, and the new position is seen as a start to the company's procurement group. This may result in more than one customer satisfaction survey being sent.

Final Report

This project has generated a large amount of information. Documentation from the project can serve as a guide to running a similar project in the future. It will provide examples of all project plans, a guide to a schedule, KPIs and metrics, as well as how the consultant did. Including the consultant hire RFP makes this documentation a comprehensive project management example for the future.

A final activity is to gather the project information into a high-level executive report so key stakeholders and secondary decision makers have a record of how the project went and what decisions were made. The report may contain:

- Executive summary
- Context of the problem
- Results of the assessment
- Recommendations and implementation decision
- Plans
- Results of the PlusDelta
- Customer surveys (if done)
- Consultant performance review (if done)

The information, written in the Five Languages, closes the circle on why there was a need for the project, how the project helped solve a problem that affected company vision, what was needed to execute the project, what financial benefit might be realized through solving the problem, how change was managed and adopted, and how the project was implemented.

With the final report written and all activities wrapped up – you are done!

Afterword

Your project was a success - now you can draw a deep breath and go on to your next project fully armed with the Five Languages.

The project examples and challenges offered in this book were used as a framework against which to show how the Five Languages of Business can be used to make decisions better and faster. Imagine them as sample scripts, remembering that every conversation is situational and depends as much on the existing relationship with the receiver as it does on the language used. Again, remember that each chapter can be used alone, pick the spot in your project that applies best and go from there.

The languages may be hard to grasp at first – they take a lot of listening, intuition, and a willingness to ask questions that seem dumb. After a bit, they will become habit. Then, you will find that clients or stakeholders greatly appreciate your ability to speak to them so that decisions and information are easy to hear and grasp.

I'm not making this up. Years of feedback and my personal experience says this is true. The ability to translate your thinking from *your* context into the Five Languages is a strength that will serve you well on the path to success!

Acknowledgements

Writing a book is straightforward but not simple and should not be done alone – it can't be. Thank you, Rob, for all the big and small things you did to support getting this book done. You know what they are.

I will be eternally grateful to the readers of my crappy first draft and that they were concerned enough to be worried how I would take their comments. I think they were afraid I would quit because of the comments!

Lummi Doc – your input as one of the best writers and English professors I know was invaluable in helping to focus my lines of thinking.

Clayton – your comments were so right on and helped me clarify my thoughts where I had skipped over a concept. Bradd – your deep knowledge of change management helped me articulate the language of Change.

To everyone that texted, emailed or called with encouragement, thank you. I cannot tell you how much that meant over the process.

Melina Young, you were and continue to be, a great voice of reason (and commas) during the editing process. You gently kept me from making this book another project management manual and focused me on what I really wanted to say. Without that input this would be a completely different book and not a better one.

John Battle is the inspiration for the book title and a primary source of wisdom for a hugely educational portion of my career - the portion where I learned the tough lessons of not knowing the Five Languages. Much of his wisdom has stuck and served me well. Thank you, John, for your insight and patience.

The final proof readers Eric, Randy, Jay and Karen were invaluable in making the final version the best it can be. All the little mistakes that happen when you have looked at a manuscript for too long were caught by your reviews.

Mariann – I miss you every day. You would totally get this book.

Chris Flett - thank you for pushing me to make this a reality.